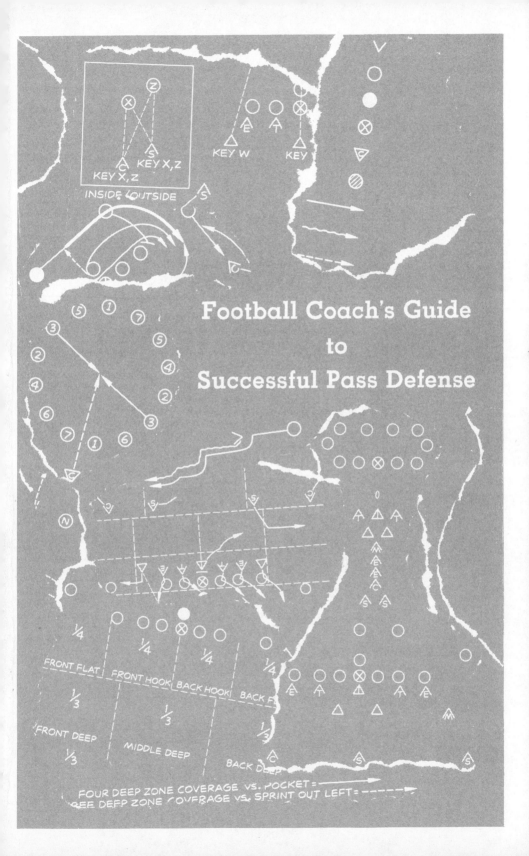

Football Coach's Guide
to
Successful Pass Defense

Football Coach's Guide
to
Successful Pass Defense

Jack Olcott

Parker Publishing Company, Inc.

West Nyack, New York

PRINTED IN THE UNITED STATES OF AMERICA

BC—O-13-324087-8

Why I Wrote This Book
and How It Can Benefit You

Teaching pass defense is the most challenging and one of the most difficult phases in coaching football today, and the coaching profession is very much in need of a handbook covering defensive secondary play.

Pass defense is more complex today than ever before because of the multiplicity of offensive formations which feature wide pro split ends, flankers, double wings, and overloaded strong spread slot backs. Therefore, the pure zone pass defense has become ineffective. With the wide pro formations, the modern pass defense must incorporate man-to-man defense vs. the isolated receiver, while other members of the defensive backfield are playing some form of zone or man-zone defense.

These wide formations have forced the defensive perimeter to make basic adjustment calls to change-up the defensive perimeter strategy so that the offense is constantly attacking a new secondary "look." The defensive secondary must be flexible enough to adjust their secondary calls "on the run." This means that specific offensive shifts, long and short motion forces the defensive quarterback to make or change his secondary call after the ball has been put into play.

Today the defensive secondary's adjustments must be more varied because today's quarterback can pick apart a straight zone or man-to-man defense. Therefore, today's zone pass defense teaching has changed from the wide cushion theory of the fifties to a type of man-zone pass defense.

The changes and innovations in pass defense have been brought about by the increased popularity of the passing game. Thus, in the last few years the defense has made more advances than the offense.

Our defensive coaching staff would prefer simplicity in our defensive pass calls, but we feel effectiveness is more important than simplicity. An effective pass defense is achieved only through the proper secondary fundamentals and basic techniques. We want our defensive program to be dynamic rather than static; therefore, our defensive secondary thinking is flexible enough to add one or two new adjustments to our basic calls each year.

Our overall football philosophy is that the defensive phase of football is more important than the offense; and, for the most part, we try to select and adapt our football personnel first to the defense.

Various successful methods of application and execution of pass defense from college, professional, and high school coaches have been integrated into our overall defensive secondary program.

The versatility and flexibility of the pass defense methods and techniques contained in this book will help to demoralize the most potent pass teams on the reader's schedule. Specific secondary alignments, depth, split rules, assignments and defensive angles are diagrammed and described in how-to-do-it terms. These will show the coach how to attack all offensive formations against the running game as well as the passing attack.

Several chapters illustrate how to correct the teaching progession and objectives for successful secondary play. Also included are advantageous teaching points on individual players' footwork, reaction, position, and confidence.

One highlight in the book is the section explaining the newest coaching secondary innovations for the "44" and "43" defenses. Also included are the different teaching and coaching methods of covering offensive motion, flood and divide pass patterns and secondary rotation, as well as explanations of how to select the defensive quarterback, how to stunt the defensive secondary, how to plan and organize pass defense practice, how to put into practice game-tested passing drills, and how to coach rushing and blitzing the passer.

The ideas and techniques on defensive secondary play in this book will stimulate the football thinking of the reader and will help strengthen his pass defense program.

Jack Olcott

Contents

17. PASS DEFENSE DRILLS (cont.)

Man-to-Man Optional Cut Drill
Inside-Outside Drill
In-Between Drill
Footwork Drills
Shadow Drill
Back Pedalling Drill
Man-on-Man Drill
Position on the Receiver
Leveling Off Drill
Offense vs. Defense Scoring Drill
Play the Ball Drill
Tip Drills
Wave—Tip Drill
Three Line Tip Drill
Head-On Tip Drill
Interception Drills
Interception Angle Drill
Dog Fight Drill
Circle Drill
Tackling
Open Field Shed—Tackle Drill
Sideline Tackling Drill
Skeleton Tackling Drill

Teaching
Pass Defense

1

In teaching pass defense, our staff realizes it is not what we know that is of importance, but rather what we are able to teach to our defenders. Each year we begin all of our defensive drills and teaching from the very beginning, assuming that our pass defenders have never been exposed to our secondary coverage system.

In teaching all of our defensive pass coverage calls, we stress the strong as well as the weak points of all our defenses. All of our secondary teaching emphasizes the whole to the part teaching philosophy. All of our players are coached to react in team and group movements, and then we drill our secondary in individual fundamentals. In our secondary group drills, everyone reacts to the same key. The key may be the passer when we are practicing our zone pass defense, while each man keys his own receiver's belt buckle in our man-to-man group and team drills.

All of our players are taught their individual responsibilities for each of their alignments for every secondary call. Through the proper coaching and continual drilling, each defender learns his individual assignment so well that he is, in turn, able to teach this assignment to a fellow teammate. He also develops the ability to react to any offensive attack smoothly, naturally, and efficiently.

Defensively we feature an attacking, penetrating defense with tight pass coverage.

As defensive coaches, we believe that we must teach pass defense in logical order to all of our deep backs. Therefore, we must convince our secondary that they know our whole philosophy behind our defensive team strategy. All of our defenders must be taught both their own individual positions and their teammates' assignments to be a complete defender. Our defensive secondary play book describes all of the fundamental techniques we use in our zone, man-to-man, and combination secondary calls. Terminology is an important chapter in our text so that all of our terms, used by all members of the coaching staff, convey the same meaning to both coaches and players.

A secondary coach should not assume that a veteran player has a particular understanding or has acquired a specific football skill because of his previous football experience.

Defensive Secondary Teaching Progression

These are the teaching steps we use in teaching our secondary defenders on the field. Defensive linebackers and ends are also taught many of the same coaching points we teach to our deeper pass defenders.

Our defensive pass drills are designed using these teaching steps as a basis for our defensive practice periods. We encourage our defensive coaches to coordinate their practice sessions so that our pass defenders will be able to practice these defensive techniques and fundamentals in group and team periods, as well as in their individual drill periods. The defensive backfield coach checks off each step as he progresses throughout early practice sessions.

I. Alignment and Position
   A. Stance
   B. Alignment
   C. Depth
   D. Moving Zones (Hash Marks and QB's Direction)
   E. Keys
   F. Play Sidelines (4 yards)
   G. All Out Speed (Sprint Action)
II. Pass Coverage
   A. Key (Potential Receivers and QB)
   B. Correct Path
   C. Play Through Receiver
   D. Maintain Leverage
   E. Catch Intercept Ball at Highest Point
   F. Play the Ball (Anticipate QB Action)
   G. Body Position

III. Run Responsibility
   A. Key
   B. Attack (Tackling Through) the Ball Carrier
   C. Pursuit Path—Correct Angle
   D. Shed Blocks
   E. Watch Ball Carrier's Belt Buckle
   F. React Full Speed to the Run (Be a Hitter)
IV. Revolving
   A. Revolve Call
   B. Talk Up Your Responsibilities
   C. Pre-Rotate
   D. Alignment and Depth (Adjustments)
   E. Change Call to Split End
   F. Explain Revolve Theory (Rotation)
 V. Three Deep Zones
   A. Locked in Three Zones (Deep)
   B. React to Ball
   C. Play Your Area or Zone First—Then to Ball
VI. Man-to-Man
   A. Maintain Leverage (Body Position)
   B. Play Ball Through Receiver
   C. Key Offensive Man's Crotch
   D. Talk Up Run to Release Man-to-Man Coverage
   E. Inside-Outside Theory
   F. Angles

Teaching Pass Defense Techniques

The blue chip pass defender must keep his eyes glued on the pass receiver until the receiver makes his final break. The defender should then tighten his cushion on the receiver, as he now can view the passer as he looks "through" the potential receiver. Once the ball is a couple of feet away from the receiver, we coach the defender to go through the receiver's head after the ball.

A sound pass defense is a talking defense. We encourage all of our pass defenders to call out an anticipated play pertaining to the opponent's formation, down, distance, or field position. Once the defender recognizes the play, he should shout, "Pass," "Reverse," or "Bootleg." The deep backs should also call out the receiver's cuts on a pass play, which helps our double coverage and under cover defenders. Since the "under" defenders often have their backs to the receivers, calling the pass cuts will help put our linebackers and other shorter pass defenders in their proper areas. The deep backs are encouraged to shout the offensive receiver's cuts because a curl call will help to direct the double covering linebacker to his inside. A sideline call warns the linebacker to begin to sprint to the outside. Since the double covering linebacker's back is often turned to the receiver, these calls are most helpful.

Importance of Our Secondary

Since most high school and college defensive backs were former offensive backs, we feel we must impress upon these boys the importance of being a member of the defensive secondary. While coaching at Boston College, eight out of our first ten defensive backs were former high school star quarterbacks! We must therefore convince these defenders that being a member of the defensive secondary is the most important position on our team. We tell our players one mistake by a deep back may result in an opponent's touchdown. The deep secondary is the last wall of defense once the opposition breaks through the line. Members of the defensive secondary are being recognized for their outstanding contributions through newspapers, radio, and television coverage. Our secondary defenders are referred to as the "Big Boys" because they must make the "Big Play" for us to win the key ball games.

Psychological Secondary Incentives

Some of the incentives we use to motivate our secondary defenders to perform consistently are:

1. No one defensive play captures the imagination of the sportswriters and fans more than the interception.
2. All of our secondary defenders who make a "big play" each week are awarded emblems on their helmets, as well as recognition on radio, television, and in the newspapers.
3. The coaching staff selects a defensive back of the week throughout our schedule.
4. We tell our pass defenders that playing pass defense is an excellent offensive weapon.

5. We emphasize the fact that only our blue chip players are chosen as defensive backs, because one mistake by any member of this group may result in an opponent's score.

Defensive Objectives for the Pass Defense

These are our five key defensive pass objectives:

1. Intercept one out of seven passes.
2. Stop the big third down play.
3. Minimize the total yards on each completion.
4. Stop the touchdown pass.
5. Don't let the opposition sustain a march with their passing attack.

Coaching Pass Defense

Pass defense must be an all out team effort consisting of all eleven men. Practice sessions help to "habitize" our defenders into their correct defensive patterns through repetition.

Our teaching philosophy is positive. When the opposition puts the ball into the air, we teach our pass defenders not only to say it is, "Ours," but to believe it through their confidence in our team defensive pass calls, techniques, and coaching points. Whenever a pass is expected, our defenders are not worried; on the contrary, we want our opponents to pass. We believe through our constant drill sessions and change-up calls that the odds for stopping the pass are on our side.

A successful pass defense takes a great deal of time by both the secondary coach and his dedicated pass defenders. The coach must sell his player into believing that he is the most outstanding defensive coach in the country. The coach must be enthusiastic about teaching pass defense, and his enthusiasm must be caught by his players rather than taught. Coaching pass defense is an enjoyable responsibility. Playing pass defense is fun and is football's most challenging assignment. All defensive football players must be made to realize that it is a privilege and a distinctive honor to be selected as a defender.

Checklist for Coaching

1. Keep the same relative position on the ball and the de-

fender next to you before and after the ball takes direction.

2. As long as the quarterback has the ball, play pass until the run develops. Whenever a running back has possession of the ball, play the run unless we key the release.

3. Always go for the ball once the pass has been thrown; take a picture and make sure you take the correct pursuit angle.

4. Always be as wide as the widest receiver and as deep as the deepest receiver.

5. Go through the receiver's head and search the receiver for the ball.

6. Stop their favorite pass patterns and make the opposition beat you left handed.

7. The defender's area becomes deeper the longer the passer holds the ball, and his zone becomes wider as the passer moves laterally.

8. The width and depth of the pass defender's cushion depends upon the speed and quickness of the receiver and the pass defender.

9. Build up the pass defender's confidence through a positive coaching approach.

Using the Stop Watch for Improving the Secondary

Throughout my coaching on both the high school and college levels, I have always been pleased at the improvement in speed a stop watch produces when introduced into any football drill. We time our secondary in sprints forward as well as backward. Timing the defender sprinting backward helps to impress upon our deep backs their improvement in their back pedalling drills. Along with their short fifteen and twenty yard backward sprints, we include a turn or two on the coach's whistle. We time each pass defender sprinting backward for fifteen yards executing one turn. A good time for this drill is 2.3 seconds.

Teaching Pass Defense Strategy

Our staff believes that the finest teaching climate takes place on a marked off football field during our daily practice sessions. The pass defense must continually react to passes with the ball on the hash marks versus drop-back, play action, and sprint-out passes. This drill gives our defense a total picture of our defensive pass coverage.

Methods of Pass Defense

We teach zone pass defense using a straight locked in zone, rotation with invert (change), and leveling off techniques. Our defensive secondary uses a straight man-to-man defense, as well as combination zone-man coverages containing inside-outside and chaser principles.

Think Pass

While many passers have a tendency to throw on third and long or second and short yardage, each passer will develop his own passing habits. A study of game films, scouting reports, and ready sheets will pinpoint certain passing tendencies on specific occasions. All of our deep defenders are always taught to think and expect a pass on each offensive maneuver.

Watch the Passer

The defender must keep his eyes on the passer looking through the potential receiver. He should never turn his back on the passer. This is why we drill our secondary men to sprint or pedal backward, keeping their eyes on the passer. The only time our pass defender will turn his back on the passer is if his man has beaten him, and then the defender must turn and sprint for the open receiver.

Once the Ball Has Been Passed, Go to the Ball

While we coach all of our players to play their particular assignment, whether man or zone, we demand all of our pass defenders to attack the ball once the ball is in the air. This is the only time we allow our defender to sprint out of his area whenever we are in any one of our zone coverage calls.

Position of Pass Defender

Position is of paramount importance to make the key interception, tackle, or break up a pass. Once the defender has the proper position on the intended receiver, he may make a real attempt for the ball by going through the potential receiver's head. The proper position is important in attacking the open field ball carrier. The defender must maintain good football position with his eyes on the target to make a successful tackle.

Charge the Ball

Just as we coach the defender to intercept the ball at its highest point, we also encourage our defender to charge the ball. This means that we must teach the defender to move toward the ball, reducing the receiver's chance of sprinting in front of the defender to make the catch.

Footwork

Along with quick hands, all pass defenders must have quick feet. Defensive coaches accomplish only what they emphasize in coaching, and our staff believes we must work on footwork drills. With the properly supervised footwork drills, a player can improve his position, balance, and quickness reactions.

Shuffle Steps

The pass defender's shuffle steps are similar to a boxer's shuffle steps. If the pass is made to the defender's one side or the other, he should push off his far foot and sprint for the ball. Once the football is in the air, we don't want the defender to take his eyes off the ball.

Pass Defense Reactions

We teach our pass defender to drop back, using shuffle steps for the first four steps, and then start using his crossover steps, keeping his eyes constantly on the passer. If the defender is forced to turn, we do not want the defender to cross over his feet because he cannot make a quick turn quickly in the direction from which he has just previously moved. The deep back's inside arm and shoulder should help to turn the defender in the direction he may wish to go. The arm movement should follow the defender's foot plant and push off the far side foot. In a couple of quick steps, the defender should be under full speed in the proper direction. The defender must face the passer so that he can get into the proper position to make the interception.

Intercept the Ball High

"Intercept the ball at its highest point" is a phrase we continually use in our coaching of the pass defenders. The defender must not wait for the ball to come down, or the receiver will beat the defender to the ball.

Tackling

Selling a defender on hard-nosed tackling takes sound teaching. In coaching tackling, we believe a defender must have had a, "I have been here before," feeling. This means we teach form tackling in a slow, step by step teaching progression before we advance to our actual hitting drills.

Teaching Recognition

To defend successfully against the pass, our defensive quarterback must be able to recognize the offensive formation and make the correct coverage call. All of the defenders must know their assignments and recognize their keys. The secondary must have the ability to move to the ball and execute the proper coverage pattern on the intended pass receiver.

While we continually change-up our secondary calls, we realize it is not a specific coverage call that is successful, but rather the ability to execute the proper technique.

Pass Defense
Calls

2

The defensive quarterback will always make a predetermined call prior to the snap of the ball. The defensive quarterback's call is based upon the offensive formation. This call determines the direction in which our secondary will revolve whenever a drop-back pocket pass develops. The straight drop-back pass calls also affect our linebackers whenever they are not called upon to blitz. We want our linebackers to drop back into their respective hook zones under normal drop-back pocket passing conditions.

We use ten basic calls by our defensive quarterback which help to determine our alignment rotation, revolving, coverage, and responsibility. The calls are as follows:

1. Single coverage
2. Change Coverage
3. Single X Coverage
4. Double Coverage
5. Double X Coverage
6. Man-to-Man Coverage
7. Combination Coverage (Man-to-Man and Zone)
8. Inside-Outside Coverage
9. Bingo (In-Out)
10. Free Coverage

Pass Coverage

Diagram 2-1 illustrates a Single Left Coverage call against wing formation with the quarterback dropping straight back in a pocket.

23

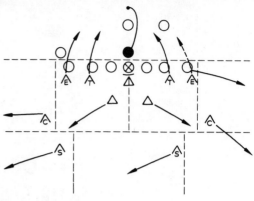

Pass Coverage vs. Wing Formation
DIAGRAM 2–1. Drop-Back Pass—*Single Left*

The left cornerback is assigned to protect the flat to his side, and he drops back on a forty-five degree angle leveling off, depending upon the depth of the first receiver's pattern. The left safety man (Strong Safety) drops back on an angle into the deep left outside one-third zone. Our right safety man (Free Safety) sprints backward into the deep middle zone as soon as he recognizes the quarterback dropping back for a pass. The right corner man is responsible for the deep outside one-third zone, while our right defensive end takes the flat zone if the near back flares or quickly veers into the flat area. Our right defensive end is taught to key the near back and to rush the passer if the back sets up to pass protect the passer. If the near back sets a course straight at one defensive end, we tell our defender to knock the back down. Once our defensive end decides to rush, we want him to run right over the blocker. Both of our linebackers drop back into their respective hook zones. While dropping back into the hook zone, we coach our linebackers to knock down any receiver who may cross our linebacker's face.

  If the quarterback rolls out to the defense's left into our Single Coverage Left call (*Diagram 2-2*), our secondary cover remains much

DIAGRAM 2–2. Sprint to Wing—*Single Left*

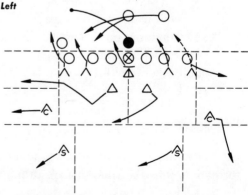

the same as *Diagram 2-1*. The exceptions are: Our linebackers begin to drop back into their hook zones but begin to revolve toward the quarterback once he has rolled outside of the guard's box. The left linebacker takes the immediate or front half of the flat zone, while our left cornerback levels off into the second half of the flat zone. The right defensive end keys the backfield flow and cautiously drops back toward the right flat zone as the quarterback begins to roll away from the defender. The defensive right end continues to revolve through the right cornerback's position if the quarterback continues to roll out crossing the line of scrimmage. Our defensive end away from the sweep would then be the deepest pursuing defender.

The defensive secondary re-revolves if the quarterback sprints or rolls away from the Single Coverage call. *Diagram 2-3* features the

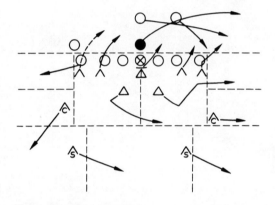

DIAGRAM 2-3. Sprint Away from Wing—*Single Left*

quarterback rolling out opposite our Single Coverage Left call. Once the quarterback breaks the imaginary line of the guard's box, our right defensive end attacks the quarterback with his outside-in contain rush. The right inside linebacker continues to key the quarterback's action and covers the first or shallow half of the defensive right flat zone. The right cornerback begins to start back to cover his deep outside one-third area but levels off into the second half of the right flat zone once he sees the quarterback's action his way. The right safety revolves his course and covers the deep outside one-third zone, while the left safety man readjusts his course to cover the deep one-third middle zone. The left cornerback starts toward his left defensive flat zone and then retreats toward the deep left outside one-third defensive zone. The left end checks for any counter action and drops off and covers the flat zone away from the backfield flow. Our left linebacker begins to drop back into his normal hook zone and keys the offensive right end.

We teach our secondary defenders to consider the pass action a roll or sprint out only if the quarterback breaks the imaginary guard box. Our secondary quarterback makes a directional call if the offensive quarterback's route is opposite of the predetermined call.

Change Coverage

We usually use a Change call toward a wide back and revolve toward the Change call. We revolve toward the call because it is often impossible for the safety to the Change side to cover a very wide split receiver on a deep outside pattern.

Our outside corner man, left corner (*Diagram 2–4*), will line up

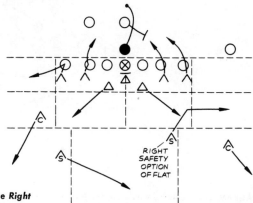

DIAGRAM 2–4. Drop-Back—Change Right

shading the wide back using his split rule for his depth and alignment, but his assigned responsibility is always the deep outside on our Change call. The safety man to the side of the Change call moves up just inside the offensive end's original position and sprints for the flat, whenever a drop-back pocket pass or a sprint-out pass toward the Change call develops (*Diagrams 2–4* and *2–5*). If action develops away from the Change call, then the safety man (left safety) away from the sprint out disregards his customary flat coverage assignment and sprints to cover the deep middle one-third zone. The left corner man away from the sprint out continues to cover his deep outside zone. The backside corner man and safety man play their normal assignments away from the Change call. If the quarterback sprints back away from the flanker's side, the Change call should be used by the safety man to the weak side and the corner man draws the same

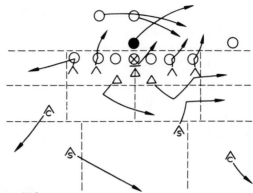

DIAGRAM 2–5. **Sprint to Strong—Change Right**

flat zone area as he did on his Single Coverage assignment (*Diagram 2-6*).

If there was a split end away from the flanker, the safety man to the split end side would make a Change call prior to the snap of the ball. He would yell to the cornerback to his side, "Change if action comes our way." Therefore, the safety man and corner man *exchange* their assignments. The safety man becomes the flat defender against the pass or the force-contain man against the run, while our corner man becomes the deep outside one-third defender or a secondary contain man against a sweep.

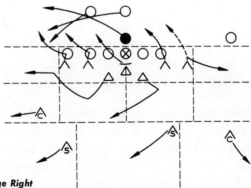

DIAGRAM 2–6. **Sprint Away—Change Right**

Occasionally we face a team that will split both of their ends. This action stretches our rotation so wide that it is impossible for the inside safety to call Single rotation to his side and still cover the deep outside zone.

Therefore, we use a Change call to the wide side of the field or toward a flanker. The safety man to the short side of the field also alerts the corner man to a possible Change call (with a split end) if action comes back toward the short side of the field. Actually we are in a semi-invert (inverted to one-half side) defensive secondary.

The Change call against the pro formations, which feature a flankerback and a split end as their two wide receivers, places the pressure on our two deep middle pass defenders. It is up to these two safety men to rotate either into the flat or the deep middle zone, depending upon the predetermined pass coverage call (pocket pass) or the sprint-out pass beyond the guard's imaginary box.

Once the Change call has been made, regardless of the quarterback's sprint-out direction or the receiver's pass patterns, our two corner men have their deep outside one-third zone responsibilities.

The Change call is usually made to the flanker's side because this is the side of the two quick receivers. On the split side we may use our linebacker in a double coverage, walk-away, stack, etc., positions to help defend against the pass to the weak side. In *Diagram 2-7* our

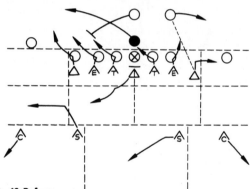

DIAGRAM 2–7. Sprint to—*Change Left*—43 Defense

defensive secondary quarterback has called Change Left and our inside safety man is assigned flat coverage. The linebacker to that side now is released to rush because he does not have to worry about the flat. This not only gives us another rusher against the pocket pass, but it also gives us another outside-in force-contain by the linebacker against the sprint out to the strong side. The left corner covers the deep outside zone, and our left safety sprints into the deep middle third. Our sprinter back is stationary and covers his deep outside area. The right linebacker covers the flat and looks for both the sideline and curl cuts of the opposition's split end.

We like to use the 43 defense against the Pro formation because it gives us one more linebacker than our Oklahoma (54) defense.

These three linebackers provide a more diversified rush and better coverage against the Pro offense.

If the quarterback sprints out opposite the call toward the split end (*Diagram 2–8*), the right linebacker is now coached to force-contain the sprint out, since he knows the free safety man will take

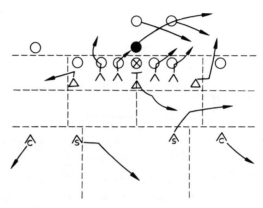

DIAGRAM 2–8.   Sprint Away—Change Right

his previously assigned flat area. If our scouting reports suggest the threat of quick passes to the halfback, we assign our right linebacker to play the halfback man to man within our Change-Zone coverage. The right corner has his deep outside zone assignment on all Change calls regardless of the quarterback's flow. The left safety man keys the quarterback's action and covers the deep middle zone, while the left corner man's assignment is the same in all Change calls. Flat then near seam is our left linebacker's assignment. He covers the flat for the quick throw-back, if the quarterback pulls up and throws quickly, then splits the left defensive seam to guard against the deeper throw-back pass. This route gives our deep secondary almost a four deep zone coverage versus the sprint-out pass. With continual practice, the two middle safety men gain confidence in their outside linebacker's deep coverage ability, and find they can favor the sprint-out side of their deep middle zone. This coverage technique has proven successful against passing teams which feature seam splitting pass routes.

The twin safety men are taught to sprint into their assigned flat zone to the side of the sprint-out pass and to favor the opponent's favorite pass pattern on a particular down and distance situation. These specific features are covered in our players' scouting reports and ready sheets, as well as during the week's daily practice periods.

Single X Call

We use our Single X Call when we want to put a safety man into our regular cornerback's position. The reasons for this shift of assignments may vary from placing a more hard-nosed defender closer to the line of scrimmage to making sure a faster man is in the regular corner position. He may be called upon to cover the deep middle zone if the quarterback sprints out away from this defender's position. If the quarterback sprints out toward the call or drops straight back, the "close" safety covers the flat (*Diagram 2-9*). The differences between our Single X call and our Change call are:

1. Single X places a defender in a stationary position to defend the corner or the flat, while our Change call runs our safety man into the position after the snap of the ball.
2. Single X is used against tighter formations, while our Change calls are usually used against the wide formations.

The revolving path of the "close" safety is similar to the inside safety man. Both defenders cover either the flat or deep midde zone.

The Single X call is used only occasionally by our defensive signal call. This call may be used as a result of an injury by one of our corner men. Thus, a team may be forced to substitute one of our deep defenders into the corner position and this call would make the substitute more comfortable in his new assignment.

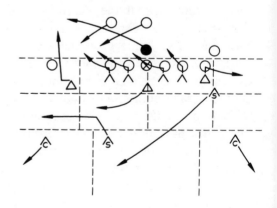

DIAGRAM 2-9. **Sprint Away—Single X**

Double Coverage

Double coverage calls are directed toward the offensive formation's power. In *Diagram 2-10* we rotate the Strong formation by

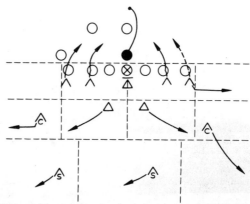

DIAGRAM 2–10. **Drop-Back Pass—*Double Left***

moving our corner man up to a "true" corner position and move our right safety man head-up on the offensive left guard's head. We still expect this defender to cover the deep right outside area because the offense is using two tight ends.

Double Left is a predetermined call, and we use the same secondary coverage whenever the quarterback sprints out in the same direction as our Double Coverage call (*Diagram 2-11*). The linebacker's routes change as the playside linebacker is taught to scallop toward the ball, and then he is responsible to cover the front half of the flat. Our playside cornerback levels off and is assigned to the back flat area. The backside linebacker is taught to key the backside hook zone. If the left offensive end breaks across the linebacker's face, he is told to knock the end down, before the ball has been put into the air. Then

DIAGRAM 2–11. **Sprint to Strong—*Double Left***

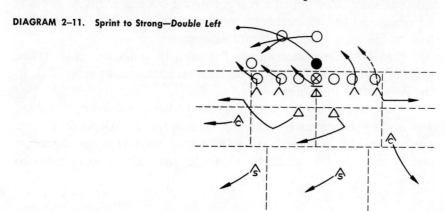

he begins to follow the quarterback's action by covering the playside hook zone. All of the other secondary defenders cover the same zones as in *Diagram 2-10*.

Diagram *2-12* illustrates a bootleg maneuver where the quarter-

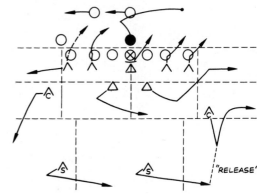

DIAGRAM 2–12.   Sprint Away—Double Left—"Release!"

back sprints out away from the Strong formation and in the opposite direction of the flow of the running backs. This bootleg action may result in a release call by our right safety man. A release call means that the right corner man is responsible for covering the deep outside zone away from the Strong formation. But with a tight end to the weak side, it is probable that the right safety man can cover the deep right outside one-third zone. Once the right safety is sure he can adequately cover that area, he gives a release call to the right corner man who now releases and covers the flat zone toward the quarterback's flow. The right corner man's responsibility is the deep outside zone until he gets his release call from the right safety. We would rather have two defenders covering the deep outside zone rather than no one.

The Strong safety begins to drop back toward the deep left out-side one-third zone until he realizes it is a bootleg play. As soon as he recognizes the quarterback's intentions, he re-revolves and sprints toward the deep middle one-third assignment.

The left corner man thinks flat until he notes the quarterback sprinting away from the call, and then he continues to drop back to the deep left outside area.

Our left end has the option on our Oklahoma defense of rushing and trailing the passer or dropping off into the flat. Depending upon our next week's opponent, we may or may not assign our defensive end, away from the quarterback's route, one definite assignment to follow.

Double X Coverage

Double X is a non-revolving three deep zone. Regardless of the quarterback's sprint out or the running back's flow, our three deep defenders are locked into a non-revolving area of responsibility.

The middle safety man's basic alignment is directly over the center, and our outside deep defenders use their regular rules or split rules to determine their alignment.

Diagram 2–13 features a straight drop-back pocket pass with our

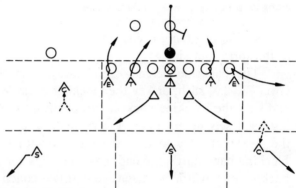

DIAGRAM 2–13.   Drop-Back Pass—*Double X Left*

secondary in a Double X Left call. The three deep defenders cover their same three deep zones in *Diagrams 2–14* and *2–15,* just as their three deep assignments in *Diagram 2–13.*

In *Diagram 2–15* the quarterback sprints out away from the Double X call and the right corner begins to move to his flat assignment. Once he realizes the quarterback is sprinting away from the flanker, he begins to drop back into the deep seam between the Strong and Free safety men. This revolving technique by our strong side corner man gives us a four deep zone against the opposition's

DIAGRAM 2–14.   Sprint to Strong—*Double X Left*

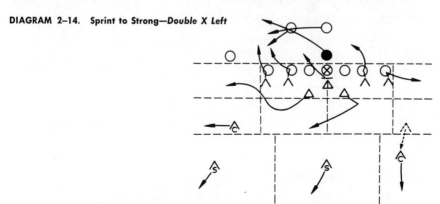

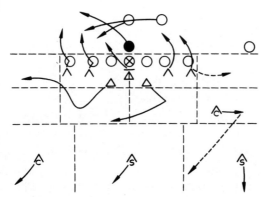

DIAGRAM 2–15. *Sprint Away—Double X Right*

passes. The revolving inside linebackers help to cover the short zones to the sprint-out side.

The backside defensive end away from the call is assigned to cover the flat, rush, or key the blocking back. Whenever the defensive end keys the blocking back, he drops off into the flat when the blocking back sets up to block. Occasionally our defensive end will rush the passer and try to take the blocker with him to the ball! If the blocking back flares, the end plays the back for a pass. If the blocking back dives toward the defensive end, we coach the end to attack the blocker and run directly over the blocking back.

Man-to-Man Coverage

Man-to-Man coverage can be used against a Strong formation, although we usually call for a zone against an overloaded offensive set. The man-to-man alignment usually shades the eligible receiver slightly to the outside or inside (*Diagram 2-16*). The depth of the

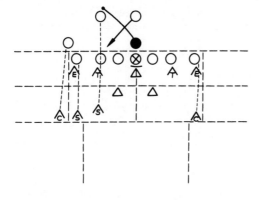

DIAGRAM 2–16. *Sprint to Strong—Man to Man*

secondary defenders appears to be staggered because the four across the board defenders move closer to the line of scrimmage when covering a back. The reason for this closer depth is that it takes the back more time to release as a pass receiver.

Both of the inside linebackers are responsible for their individual hook zones on a pocket pass.

The secondary alignment in *Diagram 2-16* sets up a possible Combination Coverage call which features both man-to-man and zone pass defense. This Combination Coverage can be a type of Inside-Outside Coverage if the eligible receivers are close enough together to make this call. Thus, we could be in a zone on one side of the field and in a man-to-man pass defense on the other side of our coverage pattern. Within this Inside-Outside call, our linebackers may be playing zone on pass plays or keying particular eligible receivers using their man-to-man assignments. Usually the Inside-Outside call would be made between our two outside defenders on the left hand side of the secondary (left corner and left safety). The right safety would play the halfback, while the right corner would key the left offensive end. One of our two inside linebackers would be assigned to play the fullback man-to-man. (See Inside-Out Coverage in Chapter 11.)

Bingo Coverage

Bingo Coverage, discussed in Chapter 7, could be used between the two safety men (Strong Side and Free Safety). The Bingo call is usually made against a Strong Flank formation to disguise our Double Coverage alignments. If the halfback would block in *Diagram 2-16,* then our Free Safety would be on his own to use his free lance technique.

Free Coverage   1545615

Free Coverage (see *Diagram 11-10* in Chapter 11) is used to take advantage of an outstanding defensive back. Whenever a coach is fortunate enough to have a player of this caliber, we feel it is a mistake not to use the defender's natural talents to his ultimate use within our zone, Free Coverage, pass defense. The free defender has the option of attacking the ball, playing a particular area, or keying a specific man. If a pass develops, our free man may use a safety blitz technique or defend against an anticipated opponent's pass.

We like to use our Free Coverage call because it does not take away the initiative from an outstanding defender.

Coverage Calls
and Alignment

3

     Diagrams 3-1 through *3-36* illustrate the specific alignments and depth of each secondary defender according to the coverage call. Each Coverage call is usually determined by the opposition's offensive formation. (Field position is an exception to the rule.)

  The depth and alignment of each defender is adjusted to the formation based upon the Coverage call of our secondary quarterback. We want to rotate our defenders, prior to the snap of the ball, to give them their most advantageous positions so they can more easily revolve after the ball has been put into play. In the large majority of diagrams, the predetermined secondary call covers two-thirds of the quarterback's action, without using a second directional call. This means that if the quarterback drops straight back into a pocket or sprints out in the direction of the predetermined call, we stay with the same call. If the quarterback sprints out in the opposite direction of the predetermined call, our quarterback makes a second revolving call in the direction of flow (once the quarterback has sprinted out beyond the "guard's box").

  In *Diagram 3-1* it is optional for the right safety to move over a

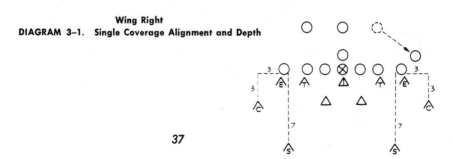

Wing Right

DIAGRAM 3-1. Single Coverage Alignment and Depth

37

couple of steps to his right to line up over, or just to the inside of, the offensive wingback, after he shifts from his previous full house set. The depth of the linebackers is basically just beyond the heels of the middle guard. This depth may vary depending upon the threat of an anticipated power run or a pass. The cornerback's position is usually three yards deep and three yards wide. Our safety men line up seven yards deep, just inside of the offensive end. At times we may ask our safeties to line up splitting the offensive end's inside foot, equidistant between the offensive end and offensive tackle or just shading the outside of the offensive tackle.

In *Diagram 3-2* "I" Right is treated much the same as a regular full house or Wing Right formation.

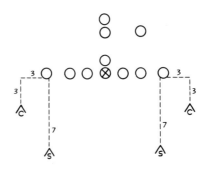

"I" Right
DIAGRAM 3-2. Single Right

If the offense comes directly out of their huddle and lines up in a Wing Right (*Diagram 3-3*) or "I" Wing Right (*Diagram 3-4*), we call Single Right Coverage and drop the left cornerback back one yard. We move the left safety just outside the offensive tackle and assign the right safety to split the inside foot of the wingback. The right corner lines up in his usual position.

Diagram 3-5 illustrates a Double Right call versus a Strong Right formation, dropping the left corner back another yard to five yards in depth and move the left safety directly over the offensive right guard's position. Double Right places the right safety head-up on the wingback, while the right corner is in the regular three-three position.

Double X Right can also be called against a Strong Right formation as shown in *Diagram 3-6*. This call locks in all three deep defenders into protecting the three deep zones, and they will never revolve out of these assignments regardless of the quarterback's action or the receivers' patterns. Just prior to the snap of the ball, our left corner moves back to a seven yard position so he can protect his outside zone. The reason we do not put him into a regular three deep

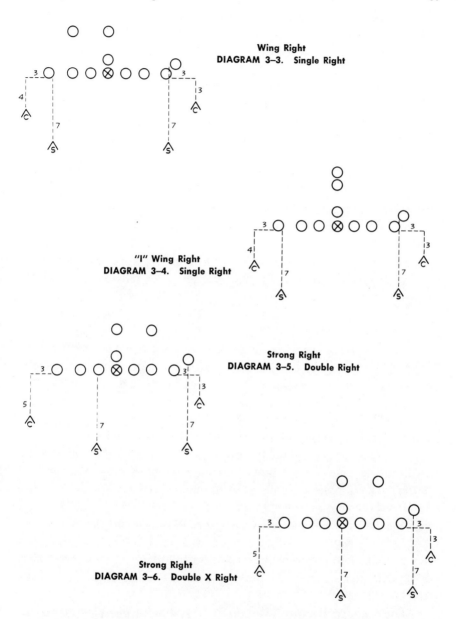

Wing Right
DIAGRAM 3–3. Single Right

"I" Wing Right
DIAGRAM 3–4. Single Right

Strong Right
DIAGRAM 3–5. Double Right

Strong Right
DIAGRAM 3–6. Double X Right

across the board alignment is that we do not want to give our secondary coverage call away too soon. This knowledge might enable the opposing quarterback to adjust his offensive call, thus taking away the advantage of our change-up, using the Double X call. We teach the defensive quarterback to do everything within his power to help take away the initiative from the offensive attack.

We use Single Coverage against both the offensive Slot Right and Break Right formation. Against the Slot Right (*Diagram 3-7*), we play our left side defenders in their normal positions and tell our right safety to split the difference between the slot and right end. The right cornerback is assigned to use his three-three rule on the right end. Against the Break Right (*Diagram 3-8*), our left side of the secondary lines up in their regular alignment and our right safety moves head-up on the wingback and the right cornerback uses his three-three rule.

The man-to-man defensive alignment often resembles an invert defense against the Break Right formation (*Diagram 3-9*) because our inside safety men's depth is less than the corner men. The reason for the difference in alignment is that our safety men do not have to be as deep versus the halfbacks because they are already lined up deep in the offensive backfield. The left cornerback's assigned man is on the line of scrimmage and the right cornerback's wingback is just off the line.

In *Diagram 3-10* we have used a Double Right call instead of a Double X call because the offense is a balanced formation. This means they have two receivers to the right and two receivers to the left. Therefore, we want to be able to re-revolve out of our Double Right call. If we decided to make a Double X call, we would lock our defenders into a non-revolvement call. We also extend our Coverage call from Single Right to Double Right because of the width of the slot. In teaching our defenders to recognize the slot formation, we compare the wide slot to a flanker formation because of their alignment and blocking and passing power and teach our defensive secondary quarterback to make his calls accordingly.

Just how well we can rotate out of our Double Right call depends upon the width of the end to the slot side. We teach our defenders that if the left offensive end splits out too wide, it will be impossible for the right safety to rotate back to the deep middle; so, we would teach our quarterback in our secondary to make a Change Right call (*Diagram 3-11*).

The Change Right (*Diagram 3-11*) enables our right safety to revolve back to the deep middle if the quarterback sprints out to our left away from our defensive call. This coverage is true regardless of how wide our right corner may have to go with the offensive slot end's split. Therefore, we are in a semi-invert "look" to the right side of our secondary and in a regular corner "look" to our left side. If the quarterback sprints out toward our call, our right safety man is respon-

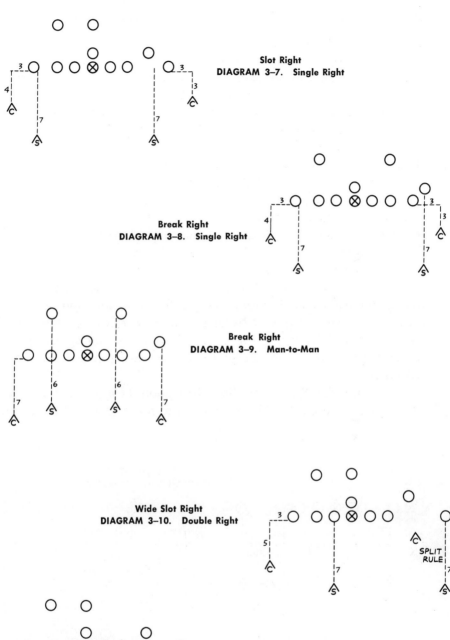

Slot Right
DIAGRAM 3–7. Single Right

Break Right
DIAGRAM 3–8. Single Right

Break Right
DIAGRAM 3–9. Man-to-Man

Wide Slot Right
DIAGRAM 3–10. Double Right

SPLIT RULE

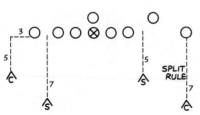

SPLIT RULE

Wide Slot Right
DIAGRAM 3–11. Change Right

sible for any eligible receiver in the flat. If the opposition runs toward the call, our right safety becomes an inside-out contain man with our right corner man also containing the sweep from the outside-in corner manner. Our Strong Side defender takes his proper pursuit angle so that he is ready for the ball carrier to attempt a cut back maneuver back toward the middle.

When the enemy uses the "I" Right split, we can call a Single Left call (*Diagram 3-12*) or a Right Change call (*Diagram 3-13*). The reason for the choice between the two secondary calls is that regardless of the call, if the quarterback sprints out to our right side, we will automatically cover a sprint out to the split end side with a Change coverage. Because prior to the snap of the ball when Single Left (*Diagram 3-12*) is called, or even if Single Right was called, the cornerback and the safety to the side of the split end use a vocal call that will place the inside defender into the flat against the pass or containing the potential sweep. So regardless of whether our defensive quarterback calls Single or Change coverage to or away from the split end, our two defenders to the split end side make an agreement to cover a sprint out toward the split end's side using invert or Change coverage.

Against the Wing Left Split formation (*Diagrams 3-14* and *3-15*), we usually call a Single Left call to make sure we have a two

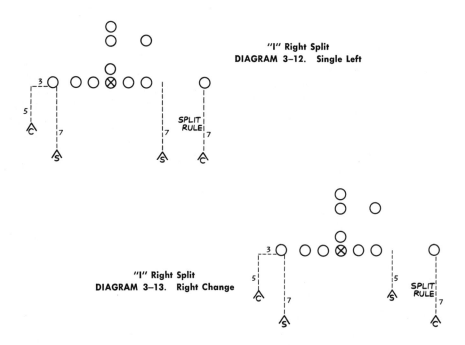

"I" Right Split
DIAGRAM 3-12. Single Left

"I" Right Split
DIAGRAM 3-13. Right Change

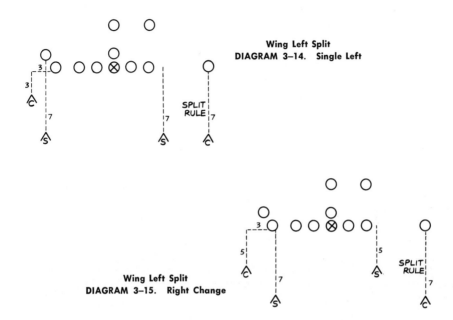

Wing Left Split
DIAGRAM 3–14.   Single Left

Wing Left Split
DIAGRAM 3–15.   Right Change

man defensive corner versus their two quick (end and wingback) receivers. If we call a Change Right to this formation, we are usually using this call as a change-up or as a particular situation where we want to get the right safety into the flat area because we expect a pass in that area. It also gives us a change-up method in attacking the sweep to the short side, because now the contain man comes from an inside-out angle rather than the customary outside-in (force-contain) method.

With each passing year, high school and college teams adopt the basic Pro formation in part or in its entirety to give their offense a "wide look." This offensive formation spreads our defensive perimeter and secondary so wide that we eliminate our Single coverage calls. We like to run a Change call (*Diagram 3–16*) toward their flanker. Occasionally we run a Change call (*Diagram 3–19*) toward their split end only when we are almost certain of a particular pass to the split side according to the opponent's tendencies. Both of these alignments are similar to our man-to-man secondary call (*Diagram 3–20*) which gives us a completely different concept of pass coverage from the Change (zone) defense.

Against a particularly strong defender, we employ double coverage techniques with the aid of our linebackers. We also use our Double

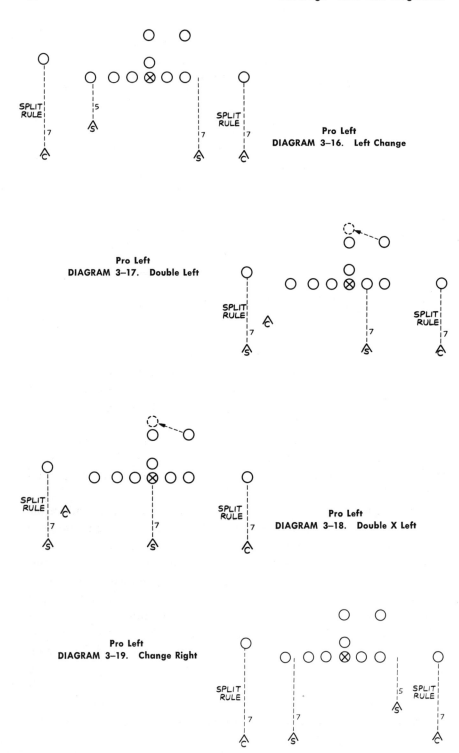

Pro Left
DIAGRAM 3–16.   Left Change

Pro Left
DIAGRAM 3–17.   Double Left

Pro Left
DIAGRAM 3–18.   Double X Left

Pro Left
DIAGRAM 3–19.   Change Right

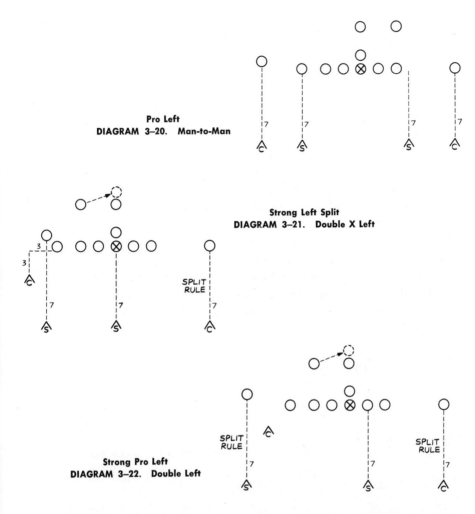

Pro Left
DIAGRAM 3–20.   Man-to-Man

Strong Left Split
DIAGRAM 3–21.   Double X Left

Strong Pro Left
DIAGRAM 3–22.   Double Left

call (*Diagram 3-17*) which allows our secondary the chance to re-volve out of our Double cover rotation. *Diagram 3-18* illustrates a Double X call which locks the three deep defenders into a three deep zone defense. The left corner man covers the strong flat, and we assign a linebacker to cover the weak flat to the split side. These stationary zone assignments simplify our secondary's assignments and help to eliminate any chance of doubt concerning the individual secondary defenders' zone or area of responsibility. Both of these Double coverage calls use just about the same alignments; thus, they help to confuse the opposition's signal caller.

Double coverage calls are the basic defensive secondary calls we use against strong formations in *Diagrams 3-21, 3-22, 3-25, 3-26.*

Double X and Double calls place our defenders to the offensive formation's strength. We also use man-to-man coverage occasionally against these formations. In using man-to-man coverage calls, we do not try to balance our defenders with two secondary defenders on each side of the center; rather, we place our defensive backs shading the offensive ends and the offensive halfbacks regardless of their alignments. Usually we assign the fullback to one of our linebackers.

Diagrams 3–23 and *3–24* feature a Double Right and Right Change calls against the Flank Right formation.

Diagrams 3–27, 3–28, and *3–29* illustrate the Break Right Flank formations with our Double Right, Double X Right, and Change Right defensive calls. The Double X call must drop off the defensive end opposite the corner man's side if the quarterback uses a straight pocket pass. The left end must cover the flat on a drop-back pass in *Diagram 3–28* because the opposition has two quick receivers eligible to the side away from the flanker. The defensive left end not only takes the flat on a drop-back pass, but is also a protective defensive device against a wide screen pass away from the right cornerback.

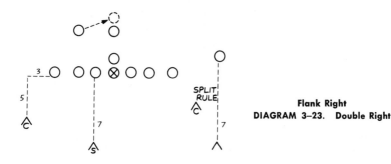

Flank Right
DIAGRAM 3–23.   Double Right

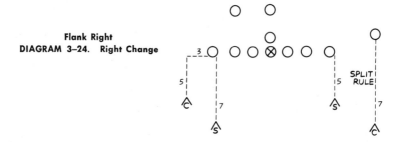

Flank Right
DIAGRAM 3–24.   Right Change

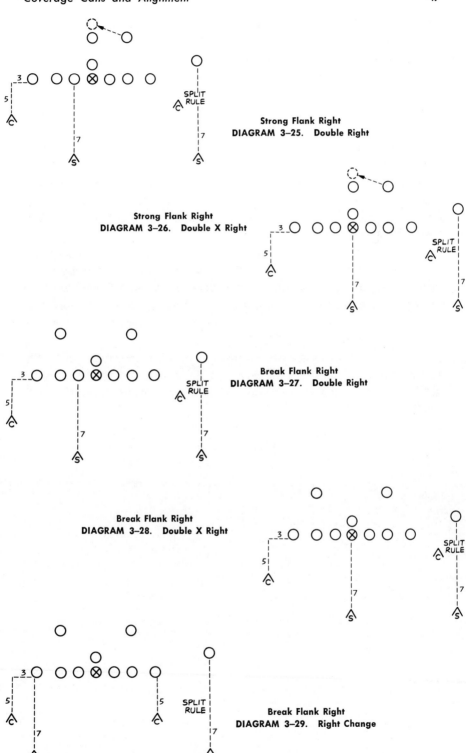

Strong Flank Right
DIAGRAM 3–25.   Double Right

Strong Flank Right
DIAGRAM 3–26.   Double X Right

Break Flank Right
DIAGRAM 3–27.   Double Right

Break Flank Right
DIAGRAM 3–28.   Double X Right

Break Flank Right
DIAGRAM 3–29.   Right Change

The Double Right call (*Diagram 3-27*) will also assign an end away from the call to cover the flat opposite the right corner. This is why we like to use our Change Right (*Diagram 3-29*) because, while we may use an invert principle toward the flanker's side, we also have a corner defense to the other side. Whenever there is not a split end opposite the flankerback, we ask the defensive end away from the call to be ready to cover the flat away from the secondary's call.

The Break Flank formation is one of the most difficult formations to defend because, if the defensive secondary rotates all the way toward the offensive flanker, it leaves the opposite side weak against passes and quick wide running strikes. This is why we teach our defensive quarterback to use his Change Right call (*Diagram 3-29*) liberally against the Break Flank set.

We use similar calls against the Pro Break formations as we do versus the Break Flank sets. Against the Pro Break formations (*Diagrams 3-30, 3-31, 3-32,* and *3-33*), however, we have the added help of our inside linebacker stationed in various defensive positions to the short side or split end's side. The Change Left is selected over the Change Right because of the threat of two quick receivers to the flanker's side. All of the calls against the Break Pro are similar to the Pro formations. The only difference is the added threat of the break halfback to the flanker's side, giving three receivers to the formation's strong side.

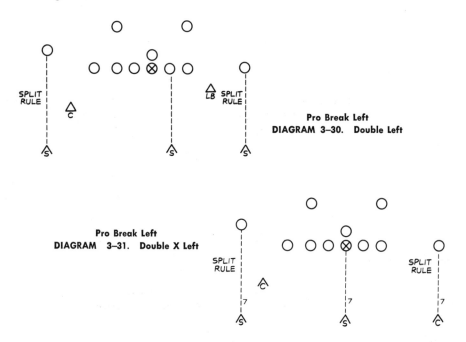

Pro Break Left
DIAGRAM 3-30.   Double Left

Pro Break Left
DIAGRAM   3-31.   Double X Left

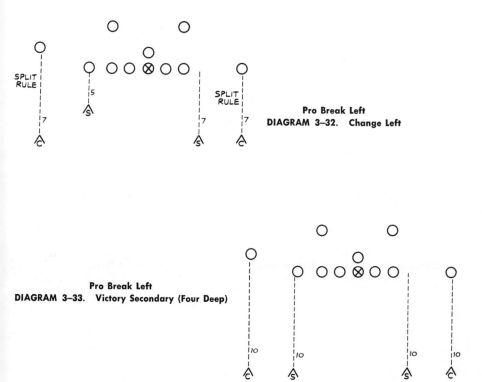

Pro Break Left
DIAGRAM 3–32.   Change Left

Pro Break Left
DIAGRAM 3–33.   Victory Secondary (Four Deep)

The four deep defensive zone coverage is used whenever we use our Victory Secondary call (*Diagram 3-33*). The Victory defense is used only when leading just prior to the end of the half or in the last few plays before the end of the game. This is a time when we expect that the opposition has no other alternative but to go for the long bomb. Therefore, we just drop back and let the opponent fire away with his barrage of long passes. This is a time we feel we can afford to give up short yardage, but we can't give the opponent the "big play."

We use a Double X call against the Strong Slot Split whenever the split is wider than five yards (*Diagram 3-34*).

If the offense sends motion (halfback) toward the split end and our secondary quarterback has called Double Left, we merely adjust our linebacker to the weak or short side (*Diagram 3-35*). We tell the linebacker to move out and play the flat zone in the direction of motion. Thus, we do not change our predetermined call or secondary's alignments or assignments.

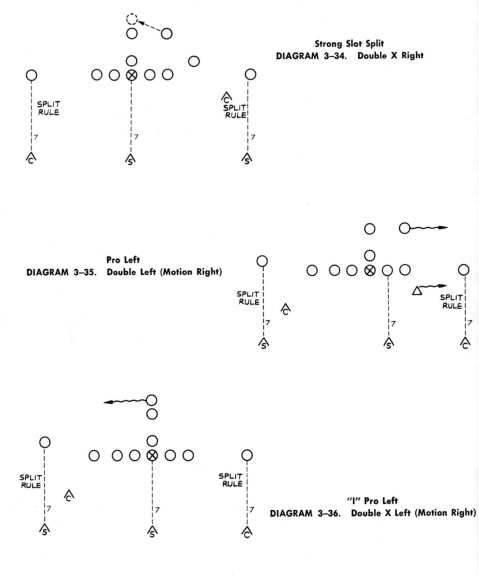

Strong Slot Split
DIAGRAM 3–34.   Double X Right

Pro Left
DIAGRAM 3–35.   Double Left (Motion Right)

"I" Pro Left
DIAGRAM 3–36.   Double X Left (Motion Right)

Whenever a man in motion sprints in the direction of our Double X coverage call or toward his flanker, we stay in our regular coverage call (*Diagram 3-36*). This means since we are in a Double X coverage, which is a zone defense, we do not have to make any defensive adjustments.

Coaching Point: Occasionally we change individual secondary defenders' positions if we wish a particular defender to defend against a specific offensive eligible receiver.

Advantages of the Double X Call

1. There are always three deep defenders in the three deep defensive pass zones without revolving into these areas.
2. There is no point of indecision against the running pass because the outside deep secondary defender is assigned the deep one-third zone all the way.
3. Deep defensive keys are cut to a minimum.
4. On a straight Double X call, there is always a deep defender in all of the three deep zones and one defender in every short one-quarter area.
5. The non-revolving, locked in, three deep defenders are a strong defense against the long pass because of the deep center fielder or safety man.
6. The call is easily adjusted to flankers and split ends.
7. The three deep Double X defenders have only one assignment to learn. The middle safety man is always the middle safety man.
8. Victory or Prevent defense uses the same three deep alignment.
9. Consistent defense against all tricky or pro formations.
10. Containment routes are the same against all formations.

Secondary
Adjustments

4

One of the most important assets in pass defense is to line up in the correct alignment so each member of the secondary can get to his coverage assignment. Our alignment is based upon our defensive linebacker's call combined with our defensive secondary captain's pass coverage call. The defender must maintain the correct alignment prior to the snap of the ball and must maintain the correct leverage and cushion on the potential pass receiver after the ball has been put into play.

Advantageous alignment and adjustments are emphasized in our players' play books, chalk talks, and throughout our daily practice sessions. We adjust our defensive personnel according to the opposition's formations as well as the opponent's personnel. To gain the proper leverage and alignment, we must train our defensive captains to be able to recognize and identify the opposition's formations.

We practice adjusting to the regular offensive formations during our spring practice and early two-a-day fall drills. Once the season begins, our scout reports any unique formations which our next week's opponents have used in the past. The scout reviews these new formations which he has seen the opposition using on film or via his scouting report.

When we face the tight or closed offensive formations, we usually rotate to the wide side of the field, prior to the snap of the ball or toward the side of the formation they have favored, according to previous scouting reports and game films. Once the ball is put into play, our secondary defensive call revolves the defenders toward the action or direction of the quarterback. If it is a straight drop-back pocket pass, our secondary carries out their predetermined call. If their tight formation has an overload of backs (more than two to one side of the center), we may move an extra man to that side and play our secondary in a three deep pattern. We have two three deep secondary calls against a strong or overloaded offensive formation. One call puts our three deep secondary defenders locked into their positions, which means they do not revolve in a lateral move but only cover their predetermined deep one-third assignment regardless of the quarterback's action. Another defensive call squirms or rotates the defensive backs in the direction of the strong side of the offensive formation. The defensive coverage now revolves, if the quarterback sprints out, away from the strong side of the formation.

Against the wide or pro formations, we have many secondary calls we can keep changing up on the quarterback to cover the wide receives. In the past we have used zone, man-to-man, change-ups (invert), and a combination of these calls. We feel it necessary to have multi-purpose defensive secondary calls to attack offensive passing formations of today. Additional linebacker adjustments, coverage, and support are necessary when covering the many splits, flankers, slots, etc. of the wide formations of today. Most of the motion adjustments are covered by our defensive backs rather than by our linebackers because we have found it is easier to adjust the deep backs just prior to the snap of the ball than it is to readjust a linebacker who may be too close to the formation to quickly shift his alignment.

The secondary's adjustment to the wide or pro formations depends upon the call. Our outside defenders are assigned a split rule whenever they are called upon to adjust their alignment. The split rule is predicated upon the secondary call, field position, and width of the potential pass receiver. (See Chapter 5 for the Split Rule.)

Whenever we are in a man-to-man defense against a wide end or back, the depth of the defender depends upon the potential receiver's speed plus the speed of the defender. Weather conditions, field position, and down and distance tendencies also may influence the defender's alignment. In adjusting our defensive back to lining up on the receiver, we teach the defender always to take away either the inside or outside cut of the receiver. This can be accomplished by lining up on the wide receiver's inside or outside. The defensive back should never line up on the receiver's nose because he gives the receiver a two way route. Through scouting and film reports, we determine the receiver's favorite pass pattern, and we coach our defender into taking away the receiver's best cut.

Since passers are throwing the ball thirty to forty times in many games, there is no such thing as a definite passing down. Therefore, we feel we must conceal our pass coverages so that the opposing quarterback will not be able to pick our pass defense apart. Our staff agrees that our coverage disguise is successful only if our defensive coach cannot predict the pass coverage prior to the snap of the ball. For film grading purposes, we keep track of our defensive quarter-back's oral calls in our pre-season scrimmages.

Today most football staffs are enlarging their staffs and are hiring coaching specialists to coach the wide receiver. There is also a trend to hire a quarterback coach whose exclusive job is to coach the signal callers. Therefore, it is only sound coaching to work on more than one method of defending against the passing game.

LEVEL COVERAGE

For a change of pace secondary coverage to the offensive split end's side, we use our level off technique. We like to use this defensive coverage pattern against the split end whose favorite pass cut is the sideline, flag, or any other outside pass pattern. We do not like to use our level technique if the split end splits out wider than ten yards. The reason for this cautious approach to a maximum split is that our inside safety man must cover the deep outside one-third, as our outside secondary defender bumps the split end and begins to slide to the outside to take away the tentative sideline or outside pass pattern.

Diagram 4-1 illustrates the level coverage call, which is used only when the quarterback flows in the direction of the split end. This sideline defensive coverage pattern is a change-up call from our usual Change pattern described earlier, or from our regular three deep zone or man-to-man pass defense.

We teach our outside halfback to bump or chug the split end and

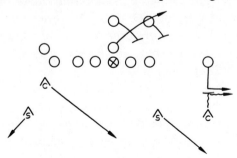

DIAGRAM 4-1. Level Off Coverage

then to slide toward the sideline whenever the level technique is used. The defender levels off once contact has been made and looks first for the sideline cut. He is taught to have an inside cushion on the split end, so that the quarterback is forced to throw the ball over the leveled off pass defender if he attempts to hit his receiver on an outside pass route. We feel that this is our best defensive secondary zone coverage call against the outside pass cut.

Teamwork is essential using our level off coverage pattern, as both our inside safety man and outside halfback must talk to one another on the run, as they cover the pass route. In the event the split end decides not to run a sideline cut and cuts to the inside, our outside defending halfback must look for a secondary receiver (near halfback or dragging backside receiver) coming into his zone. If no secondary receiver breaks into his zone, he listens for the inside safety man's directional call (curl, hook, etc.) and reacts accordingly. Actually, the halfback is free if no receiver breaks into his zone and may begin to slide to the inside, prior to the inside safety man's directional call.

The level call is a predetermined call by our secondary captain, which takes place only to the offensive end's side if the quarterback flows to that particular end's side. *The level call does not have to be called only to a split end's side.* It can also be used to the tight end's side, but we favor the call away from the flanker or wingback's side.

We teach our level off man to attack the split end and not to wait for him to make his cut. The pass defender delivers a solid blow on the split receiver and then begins to slide to the outside. The inside safety man helps our defender by calling out the pass pattern by the split receiver, if he gets behind the leveling defender. We coach our zone pass defenders to watch the quarterback's eyes and then react to the ball once the passer throws.

The tighter the end's split, the easier it is to use the level call; because, with a tight formation, our inside safety man has a shorter route to get to the deep outside one-third zone. The cornerback away from the level call covers the deep middle one-third zone versus the sprint-out pass, and our backside safety covers his normal outside one-third area (*Diagram 4-2*).

Some defensive teams attempt to use the level pass coverage strategy against teams who split their ends out fifteen yards or more; but, we feel there is a breaking point if you expect your inside safety to cover the deep outside against an exceptionally wide split receiver. Therefore, we give our defensive secondary safety a rule of thumb

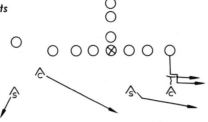

DIAGRAM 4–2. Level Off—Doubling Up

decision concerning the leverage call. If he calls a level coverage call, he is bragging that he can cover the deep outside zone because he is calling for the outside deep defender to take away the sideline pass route by leveling.

Against the curl pattern, our deep frontside safety gives the outside leveling defender an oral call, "Curl." This alerts the leveler that the anticipated outside pass route is off and that the pass receiver is curling to the inside. The leveler then begins to key the outside short zone for a delayed receiver, and he begins to slide to the inside curl man if no receiver enters his outside short zone. The reason we ask our safety man to make a call is that the intended receiver usually makes his inside curl cut after he has been held up and behind the leveling pass defender. The curl pattern may end up with both our inside linebacker and level man squeezing the split receiver with the two deep defenders, putting their hats in the receiver's back (*Diagram 4-3*).

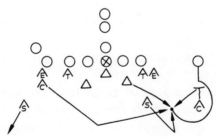

DIAGRAM 4–3. Level Off—Cover Split End's Curl

Although the outside leveler is not always successful in hitting or chugging the split receiver, his attacking leveling path forces the receiver to re-route his predetermined pass course. In order to keep the split receiver guessing, we teach the leveler to adjust his alignment and depth according to the receiver's potential and according to the score, down, and distance situations.

If the opposition runs a deep sideline pattern or the split end runs a flag cut, we coach our leveler to chug the split receiver and then to level off into the short outside zone. Once the inside safety yells, "flag" or "deep," we teach our leveling halfback to check for a delayed receiver into his zone. If no one shows, we have the leveling halfback drop back, gaining depth on a forty-five degree angle, forcing the opponent's passer to throw the ball over the halfback's head. Thus our inside safety man is afforded a better chance to make the interception.

Whenever the opposition adjusts their patterns to throw slants, quick look-ins, or short post pass routes, we keep the defensive quarterback guessing by mixing up our level cover call with change, man-to-man, and inside-outside zone man coverage calls.

MAN-TO-MAN DEFENSIVE PASS COVERING TECHNIQUES

The secondary pass defender uses a two point balanced stance with feet parallel or slightly staggered in a heel-toe relationship, depending upon our defender's individual differences. The body should be in a crouched position with the arms hanging freely just above the knees.

In man-to-man pass coverage, our defender's alignment is never head on or nose up on the potential receiver. We teach our defenders to line up on the outside or inside shoulder of the receiver, depending upon which pattern we wish to take away from the offensive receiver. We do not want our defender to line up closer than four yards to the sideline, except inside of our own fifteen yard line. If the receiver does not have a favorite pass route, we tell our defender to line up slightly outside of the receiver because he can usually get help from his inside defenders.

Once man-to-man pass coverage has been called, we want our pass defender to focus his complete attention on his assigned man. The defender is taught to ignore the first fake and to play the receiver's next moves. On the snap of the ball, we teach the defender to shuffle or back pedal backward, or to attack the receiver by sneaking up on the receiver just prior to the snap of the ball, and to chug the potential receiver on his first step. The chug is taught by using a forearm shiver into the receiver to throw off his timing. Then we coach our pass defender to play the receiver as tight as possible. How tight or close our defender plays the receiver is dependent upon whether we are blitzing the passer or playing it straight. The other reasons for how tight we play the receiver include the score, down, distance combined with the speed of the receiver, and the quickness of our defender. We teach all of our pass defenders to change up our pass coverage by attacking and playing off the receiver to disrupt the timing of the opposition's passing game.

All of our pass defenders are taught to key their respective man first, only taking a quick look at the ball once the receiver makes his final break. This is a quick look over the defender's shoulder at the last moment so that the defender can play the pass once the ball is in the air. This means the defender looks back for the ball at the same time the receiver looks for the pass. Therefore, the pass defender must be next to the receiver or slightly ahead of the pass receiver before he can glance at the ball.

The reason we stress the forward cushion on the pass receiver is that we always want our pass defender to look for the ball "through" the receiver. This means he can look at the ball and the receiver just as the receiver is about to make the catch.

There are times in man-to-man coverage when the defender will lose or get behind his man because of an offensive pick pattern, running into a fellow defender, being faked out by the receiver's move, or simply being outdistanced by a speedy receiver. When this happens, we coach our defender to forget everything else and sprint directly for the free receiver, regardless of the fact that he may have to turn his back completely on the passer.

The pass defender must maintain both a vertical and lateral cushion on the pass receiver at all times. We want our defenders to take an outside-up cushion because this places the pass defender slightly in front of the intended receiver in a position that the defender can look through the receiver at the ball. The outside-up cushion also affords the secondary defender to attack the ball through the head of the pass receiver. This cushion also places the defender in an excellent position on a sideline cut or whenever the pass receiver makes his up cut after his sideline pattern. This lateral-vertical (outside-up) cushion allows the defender to bump the receiver, throwing off the entire pass pattern. Therefore, a good lateral-vertical position gives the pass defender the best possible position to see the ball (looking through the receiver) and the position to reach any pass.

We coach our pass defenders to keep their shoulders leveled off to the goal line as long as possible versus all short pass patterns. Once the pass receiver makes his deep break down the field, we want the defender to use a cushion that will force the receiver to run into the pass defender, if our pass defender is forced to make a quick stop.

As stated previously, we want our pass defender to attack the football through the head of the receiver. The football rule book states, "A defensive player may make contact with an intended pass receiver if he makes a bona fide attempt to intercept the ball." Therefore, we coach the defender to go for the ball through the receiver's head.

Reasons We Use Man-to-Man Pass Coverage

We use our Man-to-Man pass coverage because the pass defender has only one thing to think about—his man. He is responsible for his man regardless of any offensive backfield faking by the quarterback. This coverage call moves our secondary defenders closer to the line of scrimmage, helping our overall defensive alignment stop the opposition's running attack. Man-to-Man pass defense teaches the defender to aggressively attack the potential pass receiver by playing the potential receiver closer and more hard-nosed. The Man-to-Man pass defense allows us to blitz or stunt our defenders as a change-up against the opposition's passing attack. The defensive secondary's assignments are clearer and more defined against the strong, short passing attack than they are against the zone pass defense coverage calls. When playing our Man-to-Man coverage, we help to disguise our defensive secondary's "look" so the opposition cannot predetermine if we are in a zone, man-to-man, or a combination call. Using this secondary call enables our individual secondary defender to match up against our opposition's outstanding receiver.

The free safety is a good strategy to employ when our opposition uses a minimum number of receivers to one side. We usually play some form of double coverage or zone pass defense in our Man-to-Man assignment whenever we have a free defender, as a result of a one, two, or three man offensive pass pattern. The free safety is now assigned the role of a reckless rover who is encouraged to take a chance on a pass interception. Actually the free safety man is not taking a chance going for the ball because he has been made free as his assigned receiver may not release on a pass pattern.

We use our four deep secondary because we feel the opposition will pick apart our three deep secondary if we use it exclusively. The four deep secondary gives us the best attacking angles against the running game. Since we use man-to-man coverage extensively, we want at least four defensive backs in the game at all times. With our four deep secondary, we can declare strength to a given side quickly as a result of spinning or shifting backs or a man in motion. Therefore, we do not have to adjust our linemen or linebackers as a result of a shifting or man in motion offense.

TACKLING THE PASS RECEIVER

Once the pass receiver is in position to make an apparent catch, we want our pass defender to explode through the receiver with a jolting tackle that should separate the ball from the intended receiver.

We teach our pass defenders to tackle through the receiver's numbers whenever he is executing a head-on or sideline tackle. If the defender attacks the receiver from the rear, we want our defender to explode through the neck of the pass receiver. When the receiver is forced to jump for the ball, we want our defender to cut his legs out from under the receiver. Regardless of the position of our defender, we coach him to hit the receiver with such a solid smash that the receiver will wish he had never taken up a contact sport.

The pass defender must aim his forehead through the offensive target, uncoiling from his crouched football position. As our defender hits the receiver, he forces his arms up and through the defender, wrapping his arms around the intended receiver until both of the players hit the turf.

Since all of the speed and force of the defender is going up and through the intended receiver, we want our defensive player forcing the receiver's arms apart from a bottom-up hitting position, prior to making the catch.

Once the receiver has caught the ball and is on a one on one situation with our pass defender, we want our defensive man to force the ball carrier into the sidelines. Therefore, the defender cannot afford to wait for the ball carrier; he must attack the ball. Coaching the defender to attack the runner helps to limit the ball carrier's fakes, keeping the defender on his toes rather than waiting back on his heels for the ball carrier to dictate terms. The defender is taught to tackle the ball carrier into the sidelines rather than attempt to push or block the runner out of bounds. We want our defender to tackle the ball carrier out of bounds to avoid missing him via a change of pace or cut back.

Many coaches teach the defender to take the ball carrier down any way he can get him. These coaches say they are not concerned with how many yards the runner makes, as long as the defender tackles the ball carrier. Contrary to their teaching philosophy, we coach our defenders to punish the ball carrier with a solid hard-nosed tackle. We are as concerned with the ball carrier's gaining an extra yard at midfield, as we are with his gaining an extra yard inside our five yard line. On all tackles, the defender must keep his head up, eyes on the target, shoulders parallel to the target, and feet moving on contact. We always coach our defenders to tackle through the ball carrier.

Once the first hit has been made, we want our defenders to gang tackle the ball carrier. We have learned through experience that telling our defenders to take the proper pursuit angles to the ball is not enough. All of our defensive coaches demonstrate the proper pursuit angles by showing the defenders their proper channels step by step. We always emphasize to all of our pursuing football players that they should never follow their own color. This means that each one must take a deeper and safer pursuit angle to the ball than his teammate has taken.

We coach the proper pursuit angles, correct hitting position, and follow through in our daily drills. These tackling drills are usually of the form rather than continually hitting full go each day.

PASS DEFENSE FOR DEFENSIVE ENDS

Pass Rule

"Pass Rule" is used by our defensive end whenever he is in his force position. The end's rush depends upon our secondary's pass call and the path of the quarterback just prior to his releasing the ball.

Diagram 4-4 illustrates a Single Right call in which our right

DIAGRAM 4-4. Single Right

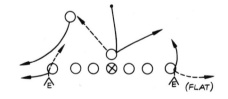

defensive end knows the cornerback to his side will cover the flat, if the passer uses a drop-back or sprint-out route toward the call; therefore, he is free to rush the passer. Our end drops off into the flat if the quarterback sprints out away from the Single Right call. The left defensive end's "Pass Play" is also diagrammed in the same illustration.

The defensive end is given these two basic principles for his "Pass Rule" assignments:

DIAGRAM 4-5. Single Left

(FLAT)

1. Call "Flat" when the defensive secondary call is away from your side.
2. When the quarterback drops straight back or sprints out away and you have called, "Flat," cover the near back to your side if he runs a flat or flare pass course (*Diagram 4-5*).

These rules are used only when we are in zone pass coverage. Whenever we are in Man-to-Man pass coverage, the ends are relieved of all their defensive pass coverage responsibilities.

Pass Key

When our defensive secondary is in a zone pass coverage, we favor the "Pass Key" call for our defensive ends. The "Pass Key" call assigns the defensive end to key the near back to his side. If the quarterback drops straight back and the near back sets up to protect the passer, we tell our defensive end to rush the quarterback. If the near back releases on his pass route, we teach our defensive end to cover the near back in a man-to-man manner. If the quarterback sprints toward the defensive end, we want our defender to use his contain-rush on the passer and to tackle him from top down. Arms extended just prior to tackling the passer forces the quarterback to throw over his out-stretched arms (*Diagram 4-6*). When the quarterback sprints away from the end and the near back goes in the same direction as the quarterback, our end is assigned to rush the passer from the backside.

If assigned to cover the near back in a man-to-man principle, we tell the end to cover the eligible pass receiver as quickly as possible to make the quarterback eat the ball or lob the ball over the defensive

Defensive End vs. Pass
1. If Secondary call is away from you, call "Flat."
2. Cover near back man-to-man if he releases on a drop-back or sprint-out away pass.
3. If near back does not release—Rush!
4. If quarterback sprints out toward you—Rush!

DIAGRAM 4-6.

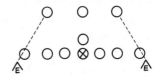

end's head. The looping pass affords the end's defensive teammates a better chance to make the interception (*Diagrams 4-7 and 4-8*).

The coaching points for the force technique are as follows:

Alignment: Split the defender's outside foot.

Stance: Two point upright stance.

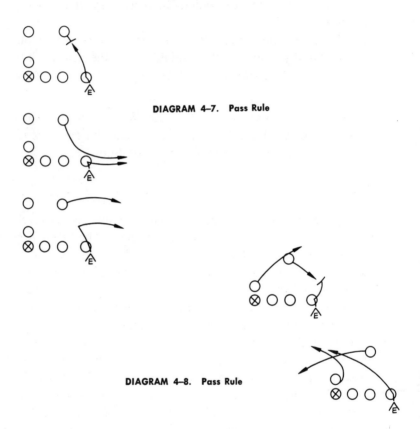

DIAGRAM 4-7. Pass Rule

DIAGRAM 4-8. Pass Rule

Coaching Points: We teach the defensive end to line up in the walk-away position and then move back to his regular force position just prior to the snap of the ball. Key the near back and use this technique only to the split end's side.

Assignment: Shoot straight for the near back. Your responsibility may be governed by "Pass Key." If the play goes away, chase the ball and do not go deeper than the ball. Never get hooked by an offensive blocker. If a drop-back or roll-out pass comes your way, rush and contain the ball carrier. When rushing, do not rush too deep or over-run the ball.

LINEBACKER'S PASS DEFENSE

The inside Oklahoma linebacker must drop back to his hook zone on all drop-back pass plays. We want our linebackers to sprint to their hook area ten to twelve yards in front of the offensive end to their side and then slide to either the inside or outside, depending upon the receiver's move. The linebackers are instructed to keep their eyes on the passer at all times while sprinting back into the hook area and until the passer releases the ball. As the linebacker sprints back on his forty-five degree angle, he keeps his eyes on the passer but is taught to deliver a blow and knock down any crossing end as soon as he crosses the linebacker's face (*Diagram 4-9*).

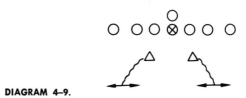

DIAGRAM 4-9.

Sprint-out, roll-out, and bootleg passes toward our linebacker force the defender to scallop deep toward the hook zone. If the quarterback continues to sprint out beyond the offensive end's original position, we want our linebacker to level off and cover the flat area. Once the quarterback puts the ball away and begins to run, our linebacker attacks the ball carrier from the inside-out or outside-in angle. The angle depends upon the linebacker's position once the quarterback decides to scramble toward the line of scrimmage (*Diagram 4-10*).

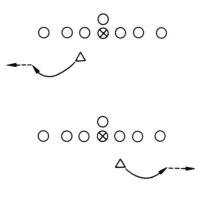

DIAGRAM 4-10.

If the quarterback sprints out away from the linebacker's position executing a roll-out or bootleg pattern, we coach our linebacker to sprint back to his backside hook area and check for the possible backside hook or throw-back pass. If the quarterback continues to roll outside of the "End's Box," sprint to the frontside hook zone; then attack the ball from the frontside hook area (*Diagram 4-11*).

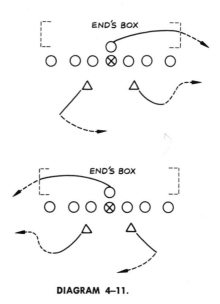

DIAGRAM 4-11.

Adjusted Position for Linebacker—Key Near Back Man-to-Man

If the linebacker is assigned to play the near back in a Man-to-Man defensive coverage pattern, we want him to rush the passer if the near back sets up to protect for the passer or goes away. When the near back flares, we teach the linebacker to attack the receiver using his Man-to-Man coverage technique. If the back releases down field, our linebacker plays him man-to-man all the way.

The linebacker in his adjusted position is a secondary contain man because the defensive end is the primary contain-rush man. The linebacker rushes or drops off versus the sprint-out passer, depending upon our previous week's scouting report. When the near back sprints away, the linebacker begins to sprint for the flat or curl area to defend against the split end. The linebacker then shifts his direction and revolves toward the deep middle zone if the quarterback sprints out away from the adjusted linebacker's position.

Walk-Away Defensive Linebacker Play

Split the difference between the split end and the offensive tackle. (Favor the tackle's side on early downs because you will be closer to where the action is.) Use a two point stance and key both the near back and the ball. We will use the end in this position if the linebacker plays his regular linebacker's position.

The linebacker is used in the walk-away position whenever a passing situation exists. Our linebacker is assigned the following responsibilities:

1. Rush and contain the quarterback's sprint outs to your side. The contain-rush technique is from the outside-in because the linebacker has an outside alignment prior to the start of the play.
2. Drop-back pass with secondary call away from defensive end's position; cover the flat or cover the deep middle zone depending upon your assignment.

DIAGRAM 4–12.

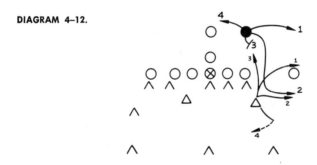

3. If bootleg action comes to your side, react in the same method as you would toward a sprint-out pass to your side.
4. If sprint-out pass develops away from your position, get into your revolve pattern.
5. Support all running plays to your side from the outside-in angle (*Diagram 4-12*).

Double
Cover Calls

5

We use double cover Split/Flank calls when our double cover linebacker covers the split end close head-up, and a defensive back is assigned to line up nose on the flankerback. The Split/Flank call means we use double coverage on both the split end and flankerback. As discussed previously, these are part of zone coverage calls, whereby the three deep defenders are locked in their three deep zones, and the Split/Flank short undercover defenders are assigned to cover the short outside zones against these two wide receivers. If flow comes their way, they immediately leave their respective zones and attack the ball. The Split/Flank nose up defenders are only assigned to cover the short zones and are not expected to cover the receivers, if they go deep or angle out of their wide flat zones (*Diagram 5-1*).

We also use a double cover "dog" call, whereby we still assign the three deep defenders to cover the deep outside three zones, while our two wide defenders are lined up on the intended receivers and are

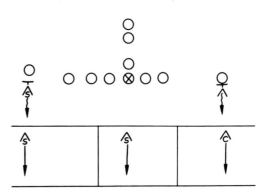

DIAGRAM 5-1. Split/Flank Coverage

69

responsible to chug and "dog" the wide receivers as they attempt to fire off the line of scrimmage. As soon as these defenders bump their assigned receivers, they are coached to play their opponents man-to-man covering the receiver deep, inside, outside, or wherever he goes. The only time these "dogging" defenders can be released is when the offense sweeps the "dogger's" way. Only then can the double covering linebacker or defensive back release his man-to-man duties to attack the offensive flow (*Diagram 5-2*).

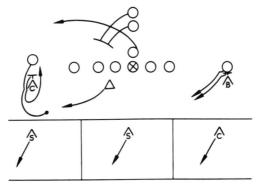

DIAGRAM 5-2. Split/Flank Coverage

The inside linebacker or linebackers may also cover the remaining setbacks in a man-to-man assignment on our "dogging" Split/Flank call. This gives us a maximum of four man-to-man under coverage, along with our three deep locked in pass defense zones.

We can also use a Split call with a man-to-man pass defense call in our deep secondary. This would place our linebacker head-up on the split end with our other four deep defenders assigned to their respective offensive receivers. The split defender may play the split end in a "dog" coverage pattern or in our normal split zone coverage. To place our linebacker nose up on the split end in our normal Oklahoma defense, we call for an Eagle alignment to the short side, with our defensive tackle and end to the split end's side moving down one man toward the center (*Diagram 5-3*).

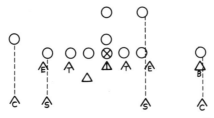

DIAGRAM 5-3. Man-to-Man with Split Call

We have also used a man-to-man pass defense with a Flank call. This places the cornerback head-up on the flankerback with single coverage on the split end. This call requires our inside linebacker to call an Eagle defense and key the near halfback if he releases for a pass (*Diagram 5-4*).

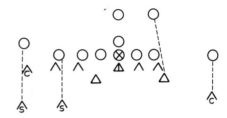

DIAGRAM 5-4. Man-to-Man with Flank Call
(Right Linebacker Keys Set Halfback)

Triple Coverage

In the past we have used triple coverage on a record breaking split end receiver. Triple coverage can be called versus an I-Pro Set defense (*Diagram 5-5*). Whenever the deep "I" tailback moves opposite

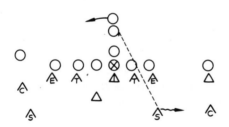

DIAGRAM 5-5. Triple Coverage on Split End

of the split end's position, it enables us to cover the split end on all pass patterns of the drop-back or sprint-out to the flankerback variety. Needless to say, we employed this defense in only strategic down, distance, and field positions. The triple coverage technique places our right linebacker one yard away and nose up on the split end, with our right cornerback also head-up on the split receiver but six yards deep. The right safety man also slides over in the direction of the outstanding split receiver. Once the tailback begins to move in the direction away from the split end, our right safety becomes free and can play the split receiver man-to-man.

If the quarterback begins to sprint out in the split end's direction, the linebacker chugs the intended receiver and then attacks the sprint-out ball carrier. As long as the tailback blocks, we may still double cover the split end with our right corner and safety defenders (*Diagram 5-6*).

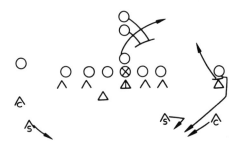

DIAGRAM 5–6. Right Linebacker Attacks Quarterback and Right Safety and Corner Double on the Split Ends.

Split Rules for Zone Defenses

Our defensive secondary's split rules are guides rather than definite dictatorial alignments. The defender's assignment, the score, the hash mark's position, the down, distance, and field position, and the eligible receiver's speed and receiving ability must all be taken into consideration to determine the defender's alignment and depth. These split rules are based upon our defensive secondary's zone calls and do not pertain to our Man-to-Man pass defensive adjustments.

Corner's Split Rule—The corner's split rules cover flankers, wingbacks and split ends. The width of these wide offensive players will determine our defensive corner's width and depth.

Split Rule:

> 5-8 yards—Play Outside Shoulder 5 yards deep
> 8-10 yards—Play Inside Shoulder 6 yards deep
> 10 + yards—Play Inside "Rule of Thumb" 7 yards deep
> (*Diagrams 5-7, 5-8, 5-9*)

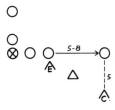

DIAGRAM 5–7.

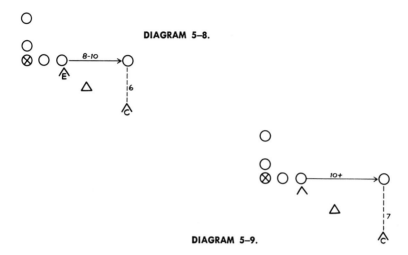

DIAGRAM 5-8.

DIAGRAM 5-9.

If the wingback's position is one to four yards away from the end, we want the corner man to play his regular width but to move up closer to the wingback (*Diagrams 5-10* and *5-11*).

If a Change call is made, the cornerback uses his split call to the

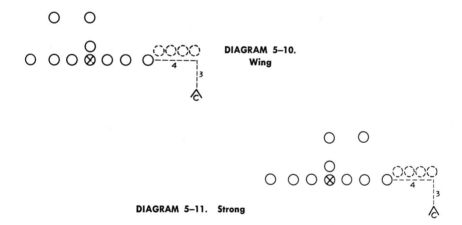

DIAGRAM 5-10.
Wing

DIAGRAM 5-11. Strong

split end's side and the safety fills the vacated area (*Diagram 5-12*).

The cornerback will also use full rotation to the flankerback if he is flanked more than five yards (*Diagram 5-13*). A Change call may also be used toward the flanker as a change-up coverage pattern.

Safety's Split Rules—The safety's split rules cover flankers, wingbacks, and split ends. The width of these wide offensive players will determine our safety's width and depth.

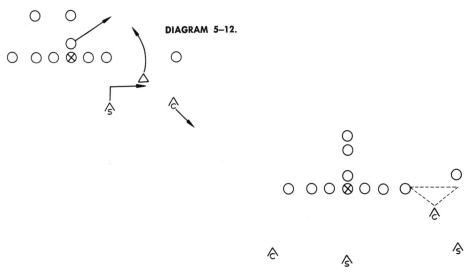

DIAGRAM 5–12.

DIAGRAM 5–13.

Split Rule:

> 5-8 yards—Play Outside Shoulder 6 yards deep
> 8-10 yards—Play Inside Shoulder 7 yards deep
> 10 + yards—Play Inside "Rule of Thumb" 8 yards deep *
> (*Diagrams 5-14, 5-15, 5-16*)

Up to a four yard split by a back we call the eligible receiver a wingback or a strong back. We teach our safety man to play the offensive back on the outside shoulder as long as the safety is sure he can still cover the deep middle zone (*Diagram 5-17*).

If a Change call is made, or whenever the quarterback sprints out toward the split end and we are in some type of a single coverage call, the safety attacks the flat zone using an invert route (*Diagrams 5-18* and *5-19*).

Split Rules for Man-to-Man Defenses

The depth of our pass defenders and their inside or outside alignment may differ from week to week. Our Man-to-Man split rules are based upon taking away what the pass receiver does best. Therefore, we encourage our man-to-man defenders to study their assigned receiver's favorite pass cut on film prior to our coming encounter.

---

* Rule of Thumb—Depends upon speed of eligible receiver, speed of defender, secondary call, field position, yard line, etc.

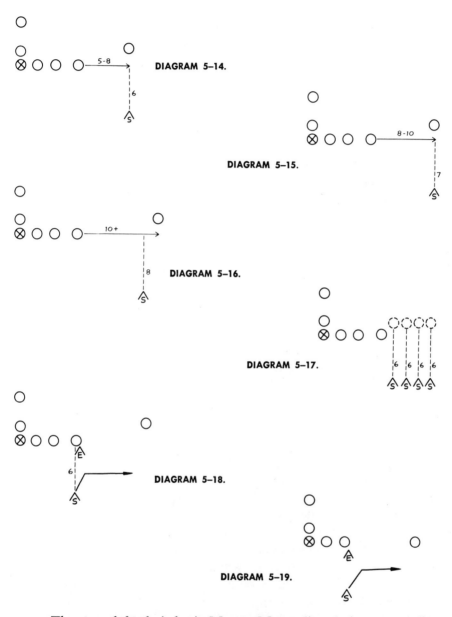

DIAGRAM 5–14.

DIAGRAM 5–15.

DIAGRAM 5–16.

DIAGRAM 5–17.

DIAGRAM 5–18.

DIAGRAM 5–19.

The pass defender's basic Man-to-Man split rule is never to line head-up on the receiver in order to avoid giving the receiver two cuts instead of taking away one of his cuts by lining up on the receiver's inside or outside shoulder.

If we anticipate a free safety man within our combination pass defense, we may urge our man-to-man defender to line up to the opponent's outside shoulder. This will often force the defender into the middle of our secondary defense where he will be picked up by our free safety man as well as his previously assigned pass defender.

Next we have compiled a chart with all of the names of the offensive formations we may face in the left hand column and the principle defensive calls we teach to our defensive secondary signal caller. This concise chart is issued to each member of the coaching staff so they may also understand our defensive secondary strategy. Along with the defensive secondary calls, we have also added a list of lettered symbols which represent the alignments of our linebackers against the offensive formation's splits, slots, wings, and flankers.

The chart is also helpful to our defensive staff in coordinating our total Defensive Program.

This compact chart, shown in *Diagram 5-20,* is frequently used by our defensive secondary coach as a quick quiz or review for his pass defenders.

DOUBLE COVERING THE SPLIT END

To reduce the number of completions against our pass defense, we use the following defensive methods:

1. Hold up or delay the receivers.
2. Rush and blitz the passer.
3. Use maximum pass coverage.
4. Continually change-up our defense by varying the above defensive techniques.

Since many schools today have adopted the professional wide open passing techniques, we feel that defensively we must use many of the pro pass coverages and techniques to contain the passing game.

If the opposition's tendency is to throw the sideline pass whenever they need the first down, we will align our defenders to take away their favorite pass cut. Our scouting report will locate their key receiver, and we will concentrate on him for the "big play." In other words, our defense will take away what the offense likes to do best; this will force our opponent to beat us "left handed" (varying from their normal attack). An example of stopping their split end's Z out pattern would be using our defensive squeeze out technique. This is a double teaming technique whereby one of our secondary defenders is assigned to the inside cushion on a Z out cut, while the other de-

OFFENSIVE FORMATIONS AND PASS COVERAGE CALLS

	Single	Change	Single X	Double	Double X	Free Safety	Man/Man
Regular Fullhouse	▷	▷				▷	▷
Wing or Slot	▷ TO	▷ TO				▷	▷
Wing or Slot				▷ TO		▷	▷
Regular Flanker		▷ TO	▷ TO		▷ TO		▷
Strong Flanker			▷ TO		▷ TO		▷
Fullhouse—Split End	Away ▷ W.A.D.	▷					▷
Wing, Slot—Split End	To wing ▷ W.A.D.			To wing ▷ W.E.D.			▷
Strong Wing, Slot—Split End				To ▷ W.A.D.			▷
Pro or Split/Backs Pro					To Flk. ▷ W.E.D.		▷
Strong Pro					To Flk. ▷ W.A.D.		▷

W = Walk-Away   A = Adjusted Position   D = Double Coverage   TO = Toward Formation   E = Eagle Adjustment

DIAGRAM 5–20.

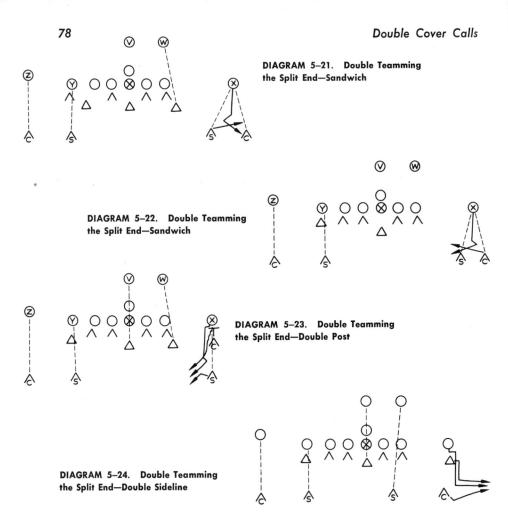

DIAGRAM 5–21. Double Teamming the Split End—Sandwich

DIAGRAM 5–22. Double Teamming the Split End—Sandwich

DIAGRAM 5–23. Double Teamming the Split End—Double Post

DIAGRAM 5–24. Double Teamming the Split End—Double Sideline

fender uses the deep squeeze method of sandwiching the defender from the back. If the split end decides to use his Z in cut, the opposite sandwiching technique would take place as in *Diagrams 5-21* and *5-22.*

In *Diagram 5-23* we double team the defender by moving our right corner man head-up on the split end, and he is assigned to chug the wide receiver and then to play him man-to-man. Our deep safety defender also plays the opponent's receiver man-to-man. Therefore, we end up in much the same sandwiching technique as in *Diagrams 5-21* and *5-22.* All of our other pass defenders play their man man-to-man with the exception of our left outside linebacker, who plays the flat zone and is assigned to pick up any receiver who enters his zone. Thus, we could end up using a double team technique if one of the strong side pass receivers runs a short flat, flare, or curl route.

If we wish to take away the split end's sideline cut, we use much the same alignment as in *Diagram 5-23,* only the right corner man (Walker) sprints off the line in a forty-five degree angle to the outside (*Diagram 5-24*). This puts the Walker linebacker in front of the receiver in the direct line of the sideline pass. This position forces the passer to throw over our linebacker allowing more time for our speeder to cover the receiver.

The outside right linebacker (Walker) follows the split end to the inside if the split end runs a look-in or diagonal route. At times we assign our linebackers to chug the receiver from either the inside or outside angle to take away the receiver's anticipated favorite cut.

Defensive Secondary
Pass Calls vs. Motion

6

Changing secondary calls based upon a man in motion can be the most confusing aspect of pass defense unless our defensive quarterback is taught a few basic and concise rules. All of the changes in the secondary calls resulting from a man in motion are based upon our predetermined call and the direction of the man in motion.

The defensive quarterback should be schooled into recognizing long motion which develops into the following offensive formation "looks":

1. Strong Formation (Motion) = Call Double X or Man-to-Man (*Diagram 6-1*).
2. Flanker Motion = Call Change, Double X, or Man-to-Man (*Diagram 6-2*).
3. Two Backs Wide to One Side = Call Double X or Man-to-Man (*Diagram 6-3*).
4. Double Wing = Call Man-to-Man (*Diagram 6-4*).
5. Flanker Wide to Split End Side = Call Double X, Man or Bingo (*Diagram 6-5*).
6. Pro Formations = Call Man-to-Man or Double X (*Diagram 6-6*).

These six suggested calls should be made once the ball has gone in motion, regardless of the predetermined pass call prior to the snap of the ball.

Using and teaching our defensive quarterback to recognize these offensive formation "looks" emphasizes the need for our signal caller

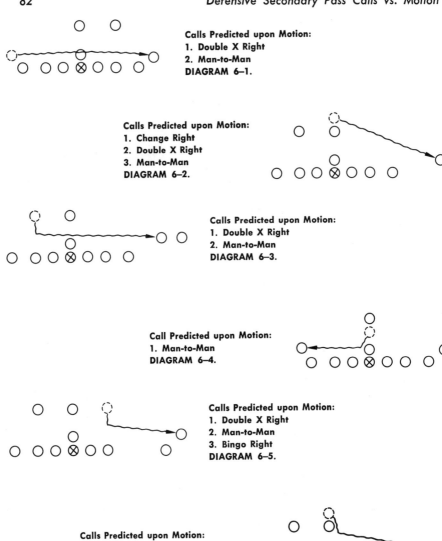

Calls Predicted upon Motion:
1. Double X Right
2. Man-to-Man
DIAGRAM 6–1.

Calls Predicted upon Motion:
1. Change Right
2. Double X Right
3. Man-to-Man
DIAGRAM 6–2.

Calls Predicted upon Motion:
1. Double X Right
2. Man-to-Man
DIAGRAM 6–3.

Call Predicted upon Motion:
1. Man-to-Man
DIAGRAM 6–4.

Calls Predicted upon Motion:
1. Double X Right
2. Man-to-Man
3. Bingo Right
DIAGRAM 6–5.

Calls Predicted upon Motion:
1. Double X Right
2. Man-to-Man
DIAGRAM 6–6.

to spend a great deal of time recognizing these "looks" via game movies, on the practice field, in chalk talks, and through visual quizzes by both the defensive secondary coach and the defensive quarterbacks.

We give our defensive secondary quarterback the chart shown in *Diagram 6-7,* which helps him to "read" the opposition's long motion.

LONG MOTION DEVELOPING INTO:

	Single	Change	Single X	Double	Double X	Free	Man-to-Man
Strong Formation					▷ TO		▷
Flanker					▷ TO		▷
Two Backs Flanked to One Side					▷ TO		▷
Pro Formation					TO FLK. ▷ W.E.D.A.		▷
Flanker Same Side As Split End					▷ TO		▷
Winger							▷

DIAGRAM 6-7.

W = Walk-Away   A = Adjusted Position   D = Double Coverage   TO = To Side of Formation   E = Eagle Adjustment

Alternate Secondary Calls vs. Motion

Some coaches favor calling secondary call changes as the man in motion begins his directional path. There are only two directions a man in motion can go: (1) Toward the center and (2) Away from the center.

For example, if a wingback begins to go in motion toward his center and continues on his path past the center, outside of the end and continues wider, the defensive signal caller may make two additional calls after his predetermined call (*Diagram 6-8*).

If the defensive quarterback has made a Double X Left Call against an "I" Left (Defensive Left) formation, he changes his call to a Double X Right Call. This keeps the motion calls consistent.

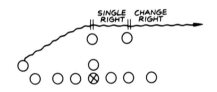

Predetermined Single Left Call
DIAGRAM 6–8.

Additional Motion Guide Rules

A man in motion may go toward the formation's strength or away from its strength. (Full house's motion is based upon a predetermined call.) Here are some coaching points that have been successfully used to determine the secondary's pass defensive calls once motion takes place.

MOTION TO (TOWARD FORMATION):

    1. Rotation Called—Stay in Rotation Call
    2. Double X Left Called—Go to Double X Right
    3. Man-to-Man Called—Stay in Man-to-Man or Go to Double X

---

* Motion opposite or away from formation is the only situation that will take us out of a Double X Call.

MOTION OPPOSITE (AWAY FROM FORMATION):

1. Rotation Called—Go to Man-to-Man
2. Double X Called—Go to Man-to-Man
3. Man-to-Man Called—Stay in Man-to-Man
4. Single X Called—Go to Man-to-Man or Single X to Motion

Man-to-Man Pass Defense vs. Motion

Basically we use a mirroring man-to-man defense. This means our individual pass defender moves along with his assigned man if his man moves in motion, and he plays his predetermined man all the way until the play is dead. Thus, a man in motion only moves one of our secondary pass defenders instead of shifting some or all of our defensive backs. We feel that simplicity is the key for man-to-man defense, and since each defender has enough to think about, this basic mirror coverage versus motion is the simplest and soundest technique.

It has been our experience that through crowd noise or misinterpretation of an oral call, changing a key from the original man assignment can cause an unnecessary amount of confusion in the defensive secondary. Some of the problems we have encountered have involved the exact time to switch to another man, wholesale secondary movement to the motion side leaving a weakness away from motion, and the offense's snapping the ball from center just as the secondary was about to make an oral shifting call.

In our mirror coverage, we coach the defender to sprint as fast as the man goes in motion and always to sprint in front of the other secondary defender, so his other teammates would not trip over the moving defender if they were backing up just prior to the pass. As the defender moves, he must maintain the same alignment and depth on the motion man as assigned prior to the motion. The defender must have his shoulders squared off to the line of scrimmage and be in a good position to play the potential receiver all the way (*Diagram 6-9*).

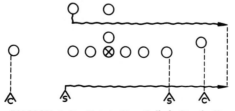

DIAGRAM 6-9. Man-to-Man Called—Stay in Man

Once our man-to-man defense has been called prior to the snap of the ball, we never change out of man-to-man coverage regardless of whether the man in motion runs to the strong or the weak side of our opponent's formation.

Alternate Man-to-Man Motion Adjustments

There is more than one way to perform any given technique or assignment in football. Our defensive motion assignment criterion is based upon the physical and mental ability of our secondary defenders. From week to week we are sometimes forced into changing our secondary coverage against a given opponent's motion because of formation or offensive or defensive personnel.

At times in our man-to-man defense, we may assign our cornerback to pick up motion to his side regardless of his previous assignment prior to motion versus two tight offensive ends (*Diagram 6–10*).

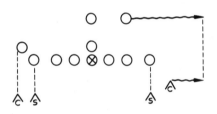

DIAGRAM 6–10. Man-to-Man Called —Stay in Man. Changing Corner/ Safety Assignment

Against the pro formation to the split end's side, we send the safety man to cover the halfback in motion because the cornerback is already split outside with man-to-man coverage on the split end. We teach the safety man to cover the man in motion running in front of the wide cornerback because the cornerback now has the entire play in front of him. If the safety man covering the man in motion takes a course behind the cornerback, there is a possibility the ball may be snapped at a time when the cornerback might back pedal into the safety man covering the offensive halfback's motion. Therefore, whenever the opposition employs a pro formation, we use straight man-to-man coverage regardless of motion (*Diagram 6–11*).

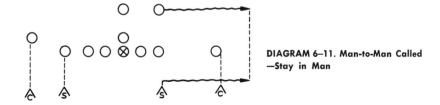

DIAGRAM 6–11. Man-to-Man Called —Stay in Man

When motion across the formation shows, we may not run our defender all of the way across the formation to play his predetermined man, but we may switch the safety man's assignment with his fellow safety man (*Diagram 6-12*). We have used a switching motion coverage whenever we have a specific safety man who is more proficient in covering a wider and faster pass receiver. Thus, our right safety man who was originally assigned to cover the inside slot receiver exchanges his assignment with our left safety. The left safety now is assigned to cover the widest man to his side on an oral switch call.

At times we have switched all of our defenders across the board because of our personnel. To keep the cornerbacks always on the outside of the formation, we have used a shifting adjustment to motion as described in *Diagram 6-13*.

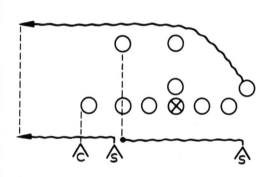

DIAGRAM 6–12. Man-to-Man Called —Stay in Man. Changing Safeties' Assignments

DIAGRAM 6–13. Man-to-Man Called —Stay in Man. Changing Assignments as Motion Man Moves

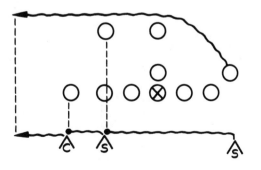

Rotation Call vs. Motion

Whenever rotation has been called prior to the play, we will stay with this call as long as the man in motion goes toward our original direction of our rotation zone call. For example, Single Right was called—we will stay in this call as long as the man in motion moves in the direction of our call, as illustrated in *Diagram 6-14*. The reasoning behind this strategy is that we have all of the deep zones and both flat zones covered.

If the man in motion would go in the opposite direction of *Diagram 6-14* toward the split end, our defensive safety man would call for Man-to-Man coverage. The reason for the Man-to-Man call is that the formation ends up in a double wing "look" (*Diagram 6-15*). We teach all of our secondary players that they must anticipate motion which may result in a Man-to-Man call. This means the defenders must predetermine their man to cover if the defensive quarterback calls for Man-to-Man coverage.

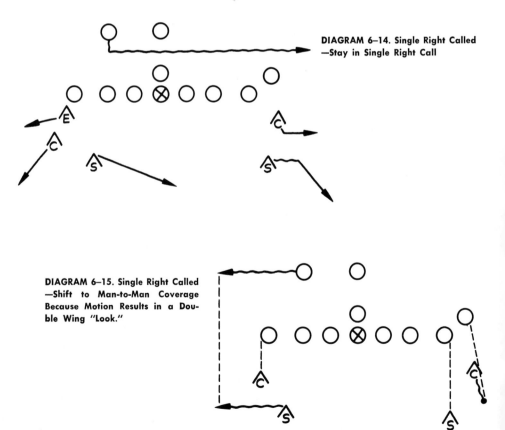

DIAGRAM 6–14. Single Right Called —Stay in Single Right Call

DIAGRAM 6–15. Single Right Called —Shift to Man-to-Man Coverage Because Motion Results in a Double Wing "Look."

Double X Call vs. Motion

When Double X is called, we will stay in that call whenever a back goes in motion toward the call side because we are locked into our zone coverage call. If the man in motion goes in the opposite direction, we teach our defensive quarterback to make a Man-to-Man pass coverage call on the run (*Diagram 6–16*). This takes us out of the locked in call and puts us into man coverage.

Diagram 6–16 illustrates how important it is for all defenders to

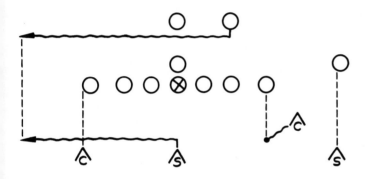

DIAGRAM 6–16. Double X Right Called—Shift to Man-to-Man Coverage Call

anticipate motion that will force the secondary into Man-to-Man coverage. Therefore, all of our defenders call out their man even though Double X coverage has been called, so that motion will not catch our secondary by surprise. The right safety keys the flanker back and our right cornerback picks up the left end. Our middle safety man keys the set halfback and picks him up as he goes in motion. This leaves our left cornerback responsible for the right offensive end.

A smooth change from a zone to man coverage can be accomplished if the first defender calls motion as soon as he recognizes a back start in motion. Once our defensive signal caller has been alerted, he makes a loud, clear, oral call, "Man-to-Man," and our defensive backs make their simple adjustments.

Single X Call vs. Motion

Depending upon our pregame strategy, we may go from our original Single X Left Call to a Single X Right Call if motion is directed away from our predetermined call, or we may go to Man-to-Man coverage.

If we decide to go to another Single X Call, we simply make two adjustments, both by our safety men. *Diagram 6–17* points out that our left safety moves back to his right taking a position behind his own left guard, while our right safety man takes a cornerback position on our right side as a result of the wingback's motion to our right side.

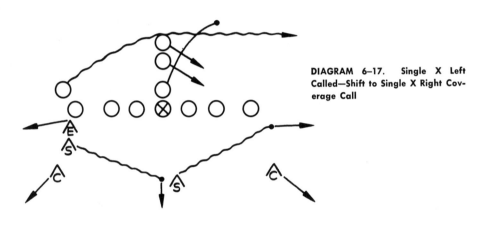

DIAGRAM 6–17.   Single X Left Called—Shift to Single X Right Coverage Call

DIAGRAM 6–18.   Single X Right Called—Rotate to Single X Left Call as Offensive Quarterback Sprints Out Away from Original Call

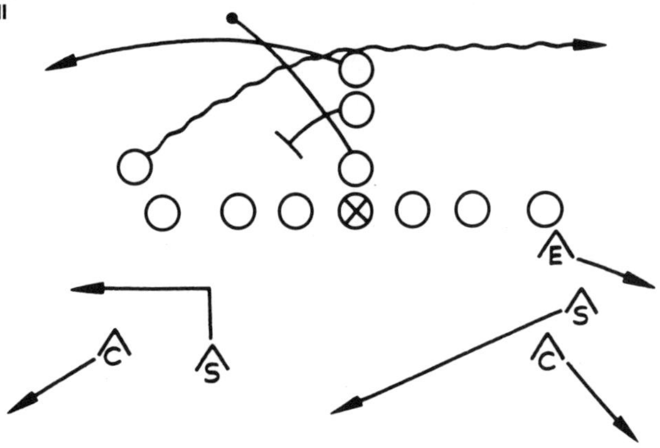

The reader may ask why not go to a Double X Right call versus this formation, but our preconceived game plan may have been cautious lest the offensive quarterback sprint out away from the motion man's direction as in *Diagram 6–18*. In a Double X Right Call, we would be forced to give up our left flat, but by using a Single X Call, we are able to rotate our safety to compensate for the sprint-out pass with a deep and flair pattern away from the man in motion.

Linebacker Covers Deep Middle

In the past we have used a man-to-man coverage on the motion man, while remaining in our customary four spoke or corner pass defense. This means whenever the "I" tailback went in motion to the strong side of the offense, the cornerback to the strong side picked up the motion man in a man-to-man assignment. In *Diagram 6–19* we have the flat to the flanker's side covered by our left safety, the man in motion is covered by our right cornerback man-to-man, and our

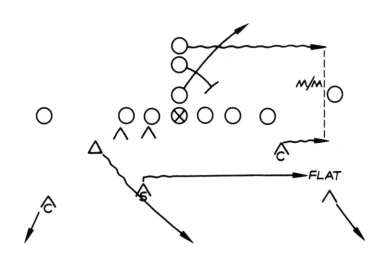

DIAGRAM 6–19. Linebacker Covers Deep Middle

two wide defensive men (left cornerback and right safety) cover their respective deep outside one-third zones. The deep middle one-third area is assigned to our walk-away left linebacker who begins to move on motion, then sprints to his deep middle zone as soon as the quarterback sprints out toward the strong side.

Goal Line
Pass Defense

7

Basically we are a man-to-man pass defensive team whenever we are in a goal line defense. We do use a zone defense within our man-to-man coverage by using our Inside-Outside secondary call. The Inside-Outside call helps to prevent confusion on the secondary's part whenever the offense decides to cross their ends or run play action passes. The inside-outside pass defense also eliminates the picking off or screening off of one of our deep pass defenders.

Along with our 65 goal line defense, we use loops and slants which are based upon previously compiled offensive tendencies. Therefore, our outside secondary defender must be able to read his keys and support from the outside against a wide play directed away from our slant or loop call. The proper alignment and keys are very important for the success of our goal line defense. Thus, we continually practice this important defensive phase throughout all of our practice sessions.

We have diagrammed our man-to-man defensive secondary alignment against the various offensive formations we expect to meet this year. While the dotted lines designate the defender's keys, we never line up directly over a potential pass receiver. The reason we shade one side or the other of the offensive receiver is that we want to take away his favorite pattern. If we have our pass defender line up directly over the receiver's nose, we give the receiver a two way pass cut.

On the goal line 65 defense, we assign our middle linebacker to the offensive fullback. He covers this back in a man-to-man assignment unless the fullback goes in motion. If the fullback goes in motion, our secondary pass defenders compensate for the motion by squirming or cheating laterally toward the fullback's direction.

We use the man-to-man pass defense against the various goal line offenses regardless of the fact that they may be of the strong or overloaded variety.

Our defenders are taught to key their respective men and to support the run quickly if their man blocks and action comes their way. If the man blocks and the quarterback drops straight back into his pocket, we want our defender to be free and attack the most dangerous receiver or roam free and go to the ball. Consequently, the defenders are taught to key their men all the way except when their key blocks —then the pass defender is coached to quickly locate the ball.

We like to use man-to-man pass coverage on the goal line because we never waste a man in an isolated area as zone coverage goal line defenses do. Our defenders are also flexible enough that we can assign our best defenders to the opposition's best pass receivers. Our scouting reports and movie breakdowns also allow us to free a particular secondary defender or several pass plays, allowing this defender to double team a specific offensive receiver. It may also free a secondary defender to attack a particular area if the opposition stays on the ground.

The depth of the pass defenders depends on how close the opponent is to our goal line. We never want our defenders standing five to six yards deep in the end zone with the ball on the two yard line. These defenders could only make a tackle in the end zone once the offensive attack cleared the line of scrimmage. Therefore, we teach our secondary defenders always to line up no deeper than their toes on the goal line. The opposition thus has only a ten yard area in depth to pass the ball and we convince our defenders that they can cover this ten yard depth if they read their keys correctly. With our secondary defenders in their proper alignment and depth, we have now four "extra linebackers" ready to attack in the event of a running play. The depth of the secondary from our ten to three yard lines depends upon the down, distance, and score.

The dotted lines in the diagrams indicate the specific key for the defenders, while the I-O stands for the inside-outside zone type of call. The defensive line slant or loops depend upon the formation's tendencies along with a coordinated line and backfield defensive calls.

Whenever the offense lines up in an "I" formation, we teach the safety to key the "I" and not only the front or back man in the "I."

The reason for this dual key is that many teams release the front man in the "I" for a quick loop or slant pass. Therefore, the safety man keys the "I" area and picks up the first man who releases for a pass.

If the offense uses a break or a split backfield (without a man in the fullback's position), we use one of our linebackers to pick up the uncovered running back. Using a linebacker to cover a "free" back enables us to cover all five potential receivers.

Correct secondary alignment is an essential step in teaching man-to-man as well as zone pass defense. Incorrect alignment may result in a touchdown pass because a defender may not have the time to react to his spot once the ball has been put into the air. Therefore, we diagram all of the offensive formations we expect our goal line defense to face throughout the entire year.

We also like the man-to-man pass defense on the goal line because the defender is only responsible for one key. The goal line pass defense must be simple enough so there will never be any indecision by our pass defenders. The reason for a concise secondary assignment is based upon the defenders' depth and reaction time. Since our secondary men must play tighter as the offense moves closer to our goal line, our defenders' reactions must be "habitized" to the opposition's key.

Diagrams 7-1 through *7-16* illustrate the defensive linemen's loops and the defensive backs' man-to-man keys and alignments. The I-O between the two deep defenders stands for inside-outside zone coverage within the overall secondary's man-to-man coverage call.

Motion on the goal line can confuse a secondary who has not practiced against this offensive maneuver repeatedly during the previous week's practice. We employ more than one method to attack motion from our secondary defense. We feel that we must attack motion in using more than one method so that the offensive team will not be sure of our defensive adjustments in advance. A multiple reacting defensive secondary versus motion often confuses the offensive strategists more than motion will ever affect the defensive secondary.

Our coaching philosophy versus motion underlines one rule—simplicity. We begin our teaching motion coverages from one predetermined call against the simplest formation and progress with the same call against the more complicated formations.

In a straight man-to-man defense, we have eliminated all shifting problems by sending the defender keying and following the offensive motion man in a man-to-man assignment. If the opposition decides to run their fullback in motion (the only back not covered by a second-

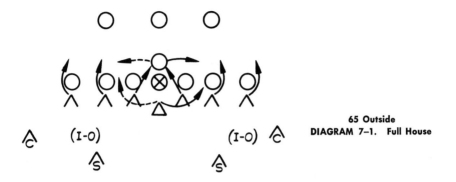

65 Outside
DIAGRAM 7–1. Full House

65 Right
DIAGRAM 7–2. Split End Left

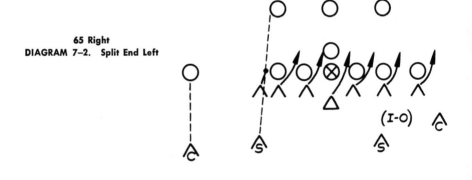

65
DIAGRAM 7–3. Wing Left

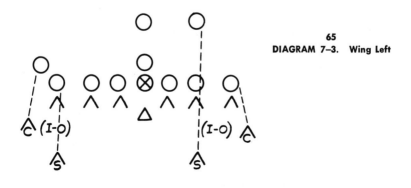

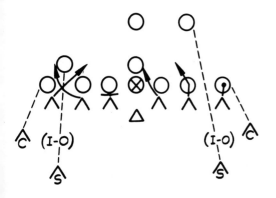

65 Cross Lucky
DIAGRAM 7-4.   Slot Left

65
DIAGRAM 7-5.   Flanker Left

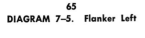

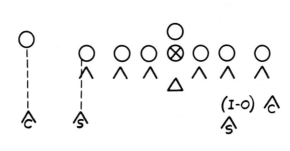

65 Right
DIAGRAM 7-6.   Strong Wing Right

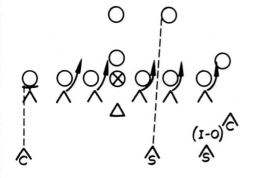

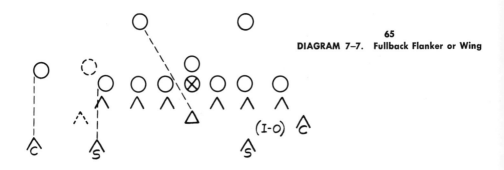

65
DIAGRAM 7–7.   Fullback Flanker or Wing

65 Left
DIAGRAM 7–8.   Strong Flanker

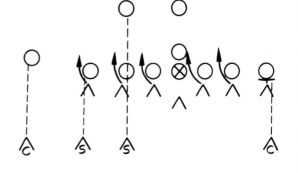

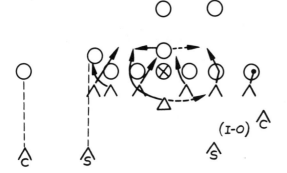

65 Key—Cross Lucky
DIAGRAM 7–9.   Wide Slot

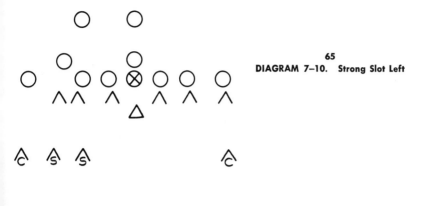

65
DIAGRAM 7–10.   Strong Slot Left

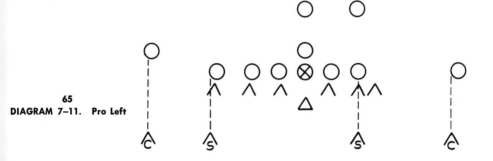

65
DIAGRAM 7–11.   Pro Left

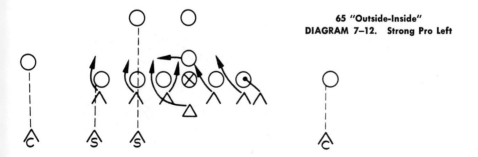

65 "Outside-Inside"
DIAGRAM 7–12.   Strong Pro Left

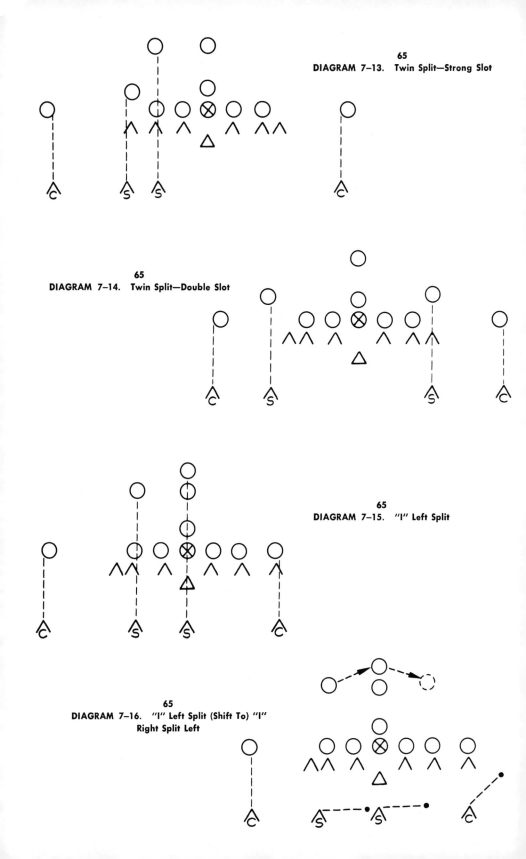

65
DIAGRAM 7–13. Twin Split—Strong Slot

65
DIAGRAM 7–14. Twin Split—Double Slot

65
DIAGRAM 7–15. "I" Left Split

65
DIAGRAM 7–16. "I" Left Split (Shift To) "I"
Right Split Left

ary defender), we assign our middle linebacker to follow him step by step. No other secondary adjustments or movements are needed to cover motion. Using our one assigned defender to cover the man in motion relieves the defense of any missed assignments or not hearing a second call once the ball has been put into play. A precautionary technique is to always run the man-to-man defender in front of his fellow defenders so that the pass defenders will not run together once the ball has been snapped. It also gives the defender who is following the motion man a better position once he has to react to a run or a quick short pass (*Diagram 7-17*).

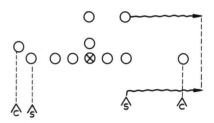

DIAGRAM 7-17. Motion—Man-to-Man

Another method of playing motion is to shift or rotate all of the secondary members as soon as motion shows, prior to the snap of the ball. If the motion would put the offensive formation into a strong formation, we would rotate our secondary around to the side of the overloaded backs and play a Double X or a straight three deep coverage with our "up" cornerback to the side of the overload (*Diagram 7-18*). This is a *Zone to Zone* coverage after motion. *Diagram 7-18*

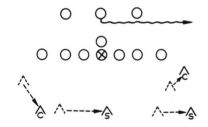

DIAGRAM 7-18. Motion—Zone (Zone to Zone)

also illustrates our right cornerback moving up to his regular cornerback position (assigned to cover the flat on a pass) as soon as our defensive quarterback shouts, "Double X Right." The right safety moves to the outside with the man in motion and is responsible for the deep right outside one-third zone. Our left safety moves from his normal position and lines up directly over the offensive center and his pass coverage zone is the deep middle one-third zone. The left corner man moves back from his regular corner position and covers the deep left outside one-third zone.

Whenever the fullback goes in motion from a regular or full house formation, and we are in our goal line man-to-man defense, the corner man and safety man away from the motion keep their same offensive men. The cornerback and the safety to the side of motion loosen up to the outside. The length of the motion determines how wide our defenders will stretch (*Diagram 7-19*). This is *Man-to-Man to Zone* coverage after motion.

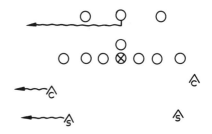

DIAGRAM 7–19. Motion—Zone (Zone to Zone)

Against the "I" formation, our assigned defender is coached to key the "I" and pick up the first man to release for a pass. If either the up back (fullback) or a deep back (tailback) should go in motion, we teach our assigned secondary defender to cover the motion man in a man-to-man assignment, unless a previous call has been assigned for a particular game (*Diagram 7-20*).

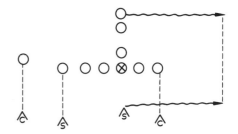

DIAGRAM 7–20. Motion (Man-to-Man)

If the halfback goes in motion away from the center (*Diagram 7-21*), the secondary shifts into man-to-man coverage. Instead of the left defensive safety moving with the motion man step by step, the corner man takes the halfback and the left safety covers the offensive right end man to man. Both the right safety and cornerbacks use an inside-outside call to cover the two quick receivers away from the man in motion (*Diagram 7-21*).

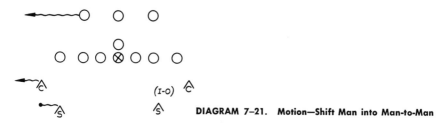

DIAGRAM 7-21. Motion—Shift Man into Man-to-Man

Against a particular team, we may designate our safety man to the side of motion to cover the man in motion regardless of his previous key. This would keep our corner man's defensive alignment consistent if the ball should come back to the same side the motion man previously vacated. *Diagram 7-22* shows the right safety covering the

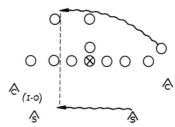

DIAGRAM 7-22. Motion Man-to-Man Safety Crosses

wingback in motion and the corner man left to defend against the left offensive end. Both the left corner and safety play the original end and halfback to their side using their inside-outside defensive assignment.

In *Diagram 7-23* the secondary slides over toward the man in

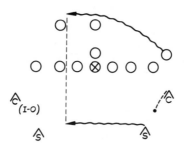

DIAGRAM 7-23. Motion Man-to-Man Shift and Slide

motion. The left corner and safety only slide toward the motion man if they are to the wide side of the field. The right corner shifts back and slightly to the inside so he can play the left offensive end man to man splitting the end's outside foot. While *Diagrams 7-22* and *7-23* are almost similar, we use both techniques, emphasizing the former with motion toward the short side of the field and the latter to the wide side of the field.

Diagram 7-24 shows the normal man-to-man coverage with the right safety man going all the way across the formation with his predetermined man-to-man assignment. All defenders play their regular assignment as diagrammed in the previous two drawings.

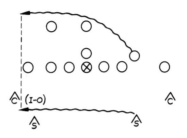

DIAGRAM 7-24.   Motion Man-to-Man (All the Way)

"Bingo" Pass Coverage

Disguising our defensive pass coverage keeps the offensive signal caller guessing. We wish to confuse the offensive quarterback by lining up our pass defenders in the same alignment and attacking a particular offensive formation in a number of different ways. In *Diagram 7-25*

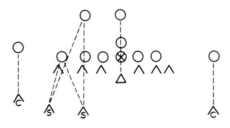

DIAGRAM 7-25.

we line up exactly as we do in our regular Man-to-Man, but we employ a change of pace coverage by using a game between our strong and free safety man. We call it "Bingo."

The inside-outside game between our strong and free safety man is similar but simpler than our inside-outside game we illustrated in Chapter 11.

"Bingo" Coverage (Diagram 7–25)

Outside (Strong Safety Man):

1. Two receivers release—Cover the outside receiver (*Diagrams 7–26, 7–27, 7–28*).
2. One receiver releases—Cover the receiver.
3. No receiver releases—Free, if flow to, force-contain.

Inside (Free Safety Man):

1. Two receivers release—Cover the inside receiver (*Diagrams 7–26, 7–27, 7–28*).

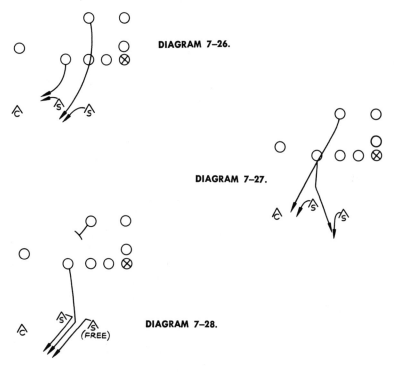

DIAGRAM 7–26.

DIAGRAM 7–27.

DIAGRAM 7–28.

2. One receiver releases—Free, roam or double up.
3. No receiver—Force, if flow to you.

Diagrams 7–26, 7–27, and *7–28* illustrate that the two safetys' coverage is actually a zone defense within their man-to-man secondary coverage. If only one receiver releases and the flow moves toward our "Bingo" coverage, we assign our outside defender (strong safety) to pick up the one receiver, while the inside defender (free safety) forces the flow from the outside. If the flow is the quarterback on a short pull up sprint-out pattern, our free safety man has the option of roaming and playing the ball.

Goal Line Pass Defense

We teach our pass defenders to play in front of their men when playing pass defense in our end zone. The old coaching adage of staying between the receiver and the goal line is naturally changed on or near the goal line. We coach our defenders to play beside the receiver, on the goal line, to stop our opponent's passing attack.

Monster
Pass Defense

Monster's Alignment Rules:

1. Go to the wide side of the field.
2. Go to the wide back.
3. Line up away from a split end.
4. Only a special defensive call will place the Monster in the middle.
5. If in doubt, go with opponent's tendencies.

Once the Monster declares his side, it gives the defense an over-shifted defense to the side of the Monster. This is the reason most Monster teams stunt and loop away from the Monster's alignment.

The reasons for using a Monster defense are:

1. Places a premium on a hard-nosed Monster who may be too slow to be a deep defensive back, not big enough to be a lineman, and not quick enough to be an inside line-backer.
2. Monster defenses adjust only one man to the offensive formation.
3. Eliminates a lot of rotation if Monster defense uses three deep secondary.
4. Gives all linemen a chance to stunt and loop.
5. Monster's main defensive pass assignment is to cover his flat zone.
6. The Monster can be assigned as both a forcing and con-taining agent.

The Monster pass defense is based upon putting the most hard-nosed secondary defender to the offensive formation's power or the wide side of the field. We line our Monster man right over the middle until the offense breaks from its huddle. Then the Monster goes to the formation side, wide side of the field, or to the side dictated by the defensive secondary call.

Since the defensive strategy behind the Monster defense is to assign the flat zone to our rugged corner man, we have also changed our other three defenders' positions according to our Monster's alignment. This means that the deep defender to the Monster's side will always be the same man, while the corner man and safety man to the opposite side will always line up in their respective positions. Other Monster teams go so far as to flip-flop their defensive ends, placing their strong end opposite the Monster, while the speed end is assigned the same side as the Monster. Using the defensive planning, the speed end to the Monster's side will always be rushing the passer on a drop-back pass, while the Monster man will be assigned to cover the flat. This type of defensive planning takes advantage of not only both types of defensive ends, but also allows the corner man away from our Monster to cover the deep outside on almost all straight drop-back passes. Therefore, the defensive Oklahoma alignment prior to the snap of the ball would look like that shown in *Diagrams 8–1A* and *8–1B*.

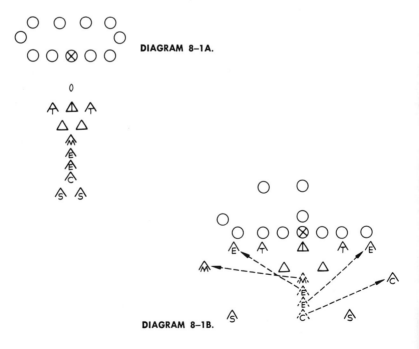

DIAGRAM 8–1A.

DIAGRAM 8–1B.

Once the offense sets up onto their offensive formation, our defensive unit breaks toward their positions depending upon the alignment of the Monster (*Diagram 8–2*).

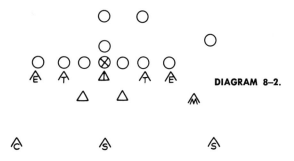

DIAGRAM 8-2.

In our defensive huddle, we always give a predetermined directional call for our pass defenders. This call is used in case the opponent would drop straight back allowing our secondary defenders a chance to revolve into some form of a three deep secondary defensive pattern.

At times we line up in a regular Oklahoma defense and play our Monster directly over the middle in between our two inside linebackers and behind the middle guard. This is a fine defense against an inside running offense. We use a three deep zone pass defense and let our middle Monster key the ball. This defense upsets the offensive blocking rules and gives the defense a strong eight man front (*Diagram 8–3*).

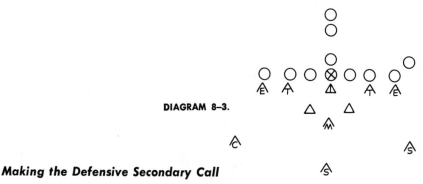

DIAGRAM 8-3.

Making the Defensive Secondary Call

In the defensive huddle, our secondary quarterback waits until after our linebacker makes his defensive call before giving his predetermined call. Once the offense breaks from the huddle and lines up into their offensive set, our defensive quarterback may wish to change his call. He must yell out his call, and all of the other secondary defenders are coached to repeat his oral call. This is an important coaching point because our defensive ends are often included in our pass defense.

After the ball is put into play, the defensive quarterback may again change his coverage call if: (1) the quarterback rolls out beyond a specific "boxed" area, and (2) if offensive motion takes place that will bring us out of our predetermined call.

Rotation Coverage

Diagram 8–4 shows the proper single coverage for all of our pass defenders against the straight drop-back pass or the sprint-out pass to

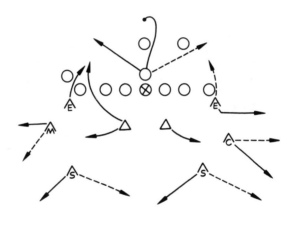

DIAGRAM 8–4.

either side. In two out of three of the actions, the Monster will have flat coverage, while his only deep outside coverage involves the sprint-out pass away from his original alignment. On this assignment the Monster man can cover his deep outside one-third zone because the passer must throw the ball a long way to hit that zone, enabling a man of average speed time to get to the ball.

    I. Drop-Back Pass
        A. Monster cover the flat.
        B. All three other secondary defenders cover their deep outside, one-third assignments.
        C. End away from Monster, cover flat.
        D. End to Monster side, rush.
        E. Linebackers cover hook zones.

II. Action Passes

    A. Corner and Monster man toward action, cover the flat. Away from action, cover the deep outside one-third area to your side.

    B. Safety men cover the deep outside one-third if pass action comes your way. Cover the deep middle one-third if action goes away from you.

    C. Ends—Action your way, contain rush. Action away, cover your flat zone.

    D. Linebackers—Action your way, cover the hook zone or rush. If action goes away, cover deep middle or hook area.

If the defense wants to keep the Monster always in the flat, even when the offense sprints out away from the Monster's alignment, the defense may decide to use the inside linebacker to cover the flat. This is another way of maintaining a three deep secondary pattern with the Monster always assigned to the flat (*Diagram 8-5*).

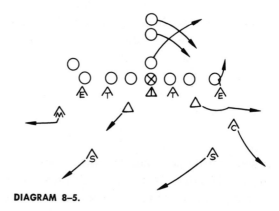

DIAGRAM 8–5.

In *Diagram 8–5* we use an Eagle call away from the Monster's position. The right linebacker flat assignment allows the end to rush the passer, not only on a sprint-out to his side, but also on a straight drop-back pass. Although this call will give up a hook zone occasionally, it is a good change-up defense and limits the coverage assignments of the deep backs. It also gives the offensive passer a different revolving look with the secondary revolving opposite the sprint-out action.

Monster teams will use a "Monster Force" at times when action shows toward the Monster man. This stunt features the contain-force blitz by the Monster and will assign an inside linebacker to cover the flat vacated by the pinching Monster man. All of the other secondary defenders rotate on the flow of the ball (*Diagram 8-6*).

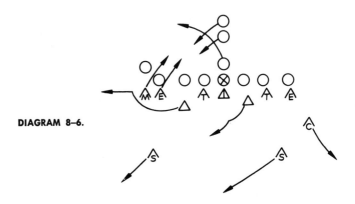

DIAGRAM 8-6.

The Eagle adjustment to the side of the force play helps to place the linebacker closer to his ultimate flat assignment. The Monster pinches on a quick move between the wingback and the end. The speed end lines head-up on the offensive end and also shoots the inside gap trying to make the quarterback make his move quickly.

If a wide receiver splits out too far for our regular rotation, it forces a Monster team to use an invert defense to the split side (*Diagram 8-7*). If the split man is employed to the Monster man's side, the Monster widens and deepens his alignment so he will be able to cover the deep outside one-third zone. The safety then replaces the Monster in the flat and the strong safety covers the deep middle zone, with the corner man dropping back into the deep outside one-third area. The only difference in this defensive coverage pattern is that the safety and the Monster man exchange coverage assignments.

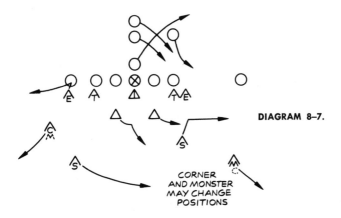

DIAGRAM 8-7.

CORNER
AND MONSTER
MAY CHANGE
POSITIONS

III. Three Deep Zones
   A. Monster—Cover flat on all action and drop-back passes. Do not attack the passer until you are sure it is a definite run.
   B. Free Safety—Cover the deep outside one-third zone on all drop-back and action passes.
   C. Strong Safety—Drop back into the deep middle zone on all passes.
   D. Corner—On all passes, cover the deep outside zone.
   E. Left Linebacker—Line up in a walk-away position and drop off into the flat on all straight drop-back passes. Play flat on sprint out your way and attack the passer only when he crosses the line of scrimmage (*Diagram 8-8*).

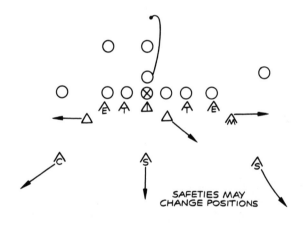

DIAGRAM 8-8.

IV. Monster's Responsibility
   A. Width and depth depends upon offensive alignment and defensive secondary call.
   B. Line up in football position. Knees slightly bent— Weight on balls of feet—Outside foot back—Semi-upright position—Parallel stance—Feet spread slightly less than shoulder's width.
   C. Reaction to ball. Drop back on a forty-five degree angle and then level off. Stay in the middle of your

zone. Keep your eye on the passer. Maintain an outside-in cushion on the deepest receiver in your zone.

    1. Drop-back passes—Cover your flat assignment.

    2. Action passes—Cover flat if action shows your way. Cover deep outside zone if action goes away from you.

D. Keys. Cue the near back through the end. Once the receivers release from the line of scrimmage, keep your eyes on the passer versus all zone pass defenses. On Man-to-Man calls, key your assigned man all the way.

E. Play the ball through the receiver's head, tackling the pass receiver high. Maintain an outside cushion on the receiver. Play the receiver slightly to the inside, six yards into the sidelines. If the receiver catches the ball in front of you, drive your head through his back and run right over him. Search the receiver for the ball from the top down. Take the proper pursuit angle to the ball.

Monster's Techniques

On power sweep we use the Monster man as a force-contain defender. This means he is assigned to force the sweep quickly while containing the ball carrier to his inside lane. His force-contain route cannot be too deep into the offensive backfield, or he can be easily blocked outside. Therefore, the Monster must keep a three yard ratio with the defensive end to his side. If the gap opens too wide between the defensive end and the Monster, the ball carrier will break loose into the secondary. The outside defensive safety is coached to support to the outside of the Monster, but he must also be ready for a cut back by the ball carrier. If an option play develops in his direction, he is assigned to contain the play by playing the pitch man all the way.

Against straight drop-back passes, the Monster's basic defensive pass assignment is to protect the flat area. When the passer sprints out in his direction, the Monster must play his flat zone first keeping an outside angle on the sprint-out passer. He cannot commit himself on the run until the quarterback has crossed the line of scrimmage.

Occasionally a corner force will be called which will signal the Monster to make a definite pinching angle toward the ball carrier. When the corner force is called, a defender will be assigned to cover the Monster's regular flat area in case a quick running pass may develop.

MONSTER DEFENSE

Monster's Assignment:

1. Key halfback through the end.
2. If ball comes your way, play flat pass coverage first, but once you determine run, contain sweep.
3. You should be our most hard-nosed defender. Punish the ball carrier with power tackling.
4. Turn all sweeps inside. Our end, near side linebacker, and safety man will help out if ball carrier cuts up inside of your containing position.
5. Meet all inside pressure with your inside forearm, stepping into the offensive blocker with your inside foot. Maintain a parallel stance so you can react to the ball carrier's path.
6. Your alignment is determined by the strong side of the offensive formation.
7. Once the end releases on a pass pattern, pick up the halfback's pattern.
8. On outside passes (sideline, veer outs, etc.), make sure you stay in your correct line with the passer. Make him throw the ball over you on outside cuts to give the safety man a chance at the interception.
9. Don't widen too much on your defensive pass course if the quarterback sprints out away from you.
10. If a zone pass defense has been called, make sure you keep your eyes on the passer as you retreat to cover your zone.

Monster's Reactions

If the ball goes straight back (pocket pass), the Monster man should drop off and cover the flat to his side, if the call is to his side.

As the Monster man sprints back into his flat assignment (ten yards in depth), he should be keying the passer over his inside shoulder as he sprints back into the middle of his zone.

As the ball goes away from the Monster, he begins to drop back into his flat area. As soon as the ball carrier sprints out past the "Tackle Box," the Monster is taught to check for any throw-back or transcontinental patterns. The Monster then begins to slide closer to the ball as the ball keeps moving away from the Monster's Zone.

If the ball moves toward the Monster, he is assigned to cover his flat area until he recognizes the play is a definite sweep. Then he is coached to contain the sweep, forcing the ball carrier to cut the play up as soon as possible. The contain-force method shuts off the ball carrier's outside route and makes him turn up through the off tackle area. This maneuver by the Monster man turns the ball carrier back into the rapidly pursuing defenders.

The Three Deep
Coverage Attack

9

With the increased interest in the Notre
Dame 40 defense, the split six and the entire eight man frontal alignments, the three deep solid zone and revolving secondary defenses
have recently gained a great deal of popularity.

These eight man front defenses depend upon a strong rush, holding up receivers and primarily zone pass defenses to disrupt the timing
of the pass patterns.

The three man zone principle is to stay as deep as the deepest
receiver and as wide as the widest receiver. Therefore, our pass defenders and perimeter contain man force the ball or the ball carrier
into the middle of the field and attack from an outside-in position.

The defensive secondary is taught to eliminate the long bomb,
intercept the ball at its highest level, and to attack and punish the
receiver or the ball carrier. All pass defenders must know the games'
tactical situations and play the pass first and the run second. When
possible we want the defender to intercept the pass. If the interception
is impossible, we want the defender to break up the pass.

Basically the eight man front defenses are zone pass defenses, but
there are times when the offensive formation or its pass patterns force
the eight man front defenses into man-to-man coverage. While the
eight man front dictates a large percentage of zone pass defense, it is
possible to continually vary the zone coverage patterns if the opposition detects a weakness in a particular zone coverage.

The most important rule we teach our zone pass defenders is to
maintain the proper balance and relationship to one another within

our zone coverage pattern, regardless of the width or depth of the zones. Each defender is taught to realize that the depth and the width of all zones never remain constant because of field position, time the passer has to throw, and the maneuverability of the passer. Therefore, we stress the fact that each defender must sprint to the middle of his zone and make sure he is as deep as the deepest receiver in his zone.

We use the following teaching progression to coach our pass defense in our practice sessions throughout the entire year:

PLAY THE BALL SEQUENCE

This is our ten point teaching progression we use to coach our defensive linebackers and secondary.

1. Alignment
2. Stance
3. Secondary Call
4. Assignment
5. Keys
6. "Take a Picture"
7. Angle of Movement
8. Concentrate on the Ball
9. Sprint to Your Zone
10. Attack the Ball

Alignment

The halfbacks line up eight yards deep and three yards outside the defensive end. Against the split ends or wide flankers, the width of the halfback is determined by the width of the widest potential receiver. The depth is determined by the formation, score, field position against wide formations. Our halfbacks are coached to play on the inside or outside of the eligible receivers up to seven yards. From this point to the sidelines, we teach the defender to split the wide man's inside foot so that the defender can maintain inside leverage on the receiver breaking toward the middle. We never want our defender to play closer than six yards to the sidelines until the passer throws the ball.

The middle safety man alignment is head up on the ball and ten yards deep. The depth of this position will increase vertically depending upon the width of the formation, score, time, field position, etc. The alignment of the safety will change only a yard or two laterally if the opponent uses an unbalanced line or a strong formation. If the ball is on a hash mark, we want our safety man to move over the offensive guard's outside foot to the wide side of the field.

Stance

Halfbacks should be in a balanced football position just prior to the snap of the ball. The defender's knees should be flexed, with most of his weight on the balls of his feet. The arms should hang down freely just above his knees. His feet should be parallel and staggered slightly, with his outside foot slightly behind the inside foot. When the ball is put into play, the secondary defender should take a shuffle step backward transferring his weight to his back foot, "take a picture" of the action, and react.

When playing man-to-man off of the three deep alignment, the stance is similar, but the feet are in a more parallel stance with the weight evenly divided between both feet.

The safety man should assume a football position as soon as the center approaches the ball. His knees should be flexed with most of the weight on the balls of his feet. The arms should hang down freely just above the knees. His feet can be staggered or parallel. When the ball is put into play, he should take a slight step backward (shuffle step) placing most of the weight on the rear foot, "take a picture" of the action, and react.

When the safety is assigned to play man-to-man defense, he uses more of a parallel stance and keeps the weight evenly divided between his two feet.

If he is in one of his three assigned zone defenses and the ball is on the hash mark, he uses a more open stance toward the wide side of the field.

Secondary Calls

The secondary rotation and revolving calls are made by our defensive secondary captain who is our middle safety man. Usually he uses oral calls, but he also has a set of signals he uses in the event the crowd noise is too loud to hear his verbal calls. Our coverage calls are basically dependent upon the alignment of the opponent's formation. Field position, time, down, distance, and the score all effect our final secondary coverage calls.

Keys

Halfbacks are taught to key the halfback through the end versus a full house. Against a slot, strong or wing, we want our halfbacks to key the halfback, the end, then the ball. If a wide man shows to his side, we want the halfback to key the ball, then locate the deepest man in his zone. Often the more experienced halfbacks are able to pick up the guards and tackles crossing the line of scrimmage indicating a definite running maneuver.

The safety is taught to key the ball and is able to pick up the center and both guards in his view. If he is assigned to revolve in any direction, he then picks up the deepest receiver in his area. We always caution our safety man to be aware of the play action and halfback passes.

"Take a Picture"

Once the defender has read his keys, we want him to "take a picture" of the quarterback's action and to react according to the secondary's call or the quarterback's course.

Although we list keying, "taking a picture," and angle of movement separately, they could all be grouped together under reaction. All three of these coverage phases must be accomplished within a split second. Therefore, our daily drill and reaction period are set up to train our defender to accomplish all of these phases as second nature.

Zone Coverage

The blitzing stunts and our line forcing unit must minimize the amount of time the offensive quarterback has to set up and throw the pass. These rushers' assignments are to hurry and disrupt the timing of the total pass pattern.

In order to get the best zone coverage against the passing attack, our deep secondary defensive areas are broken down into deep thirds, while the defensive ends and linebackers cover the hook and flat zones into fourths. These pass defenders cover their areas using lateral and vertical routes to gain their objectives.

The three deep defense divides the field in four short zones and three deep zones. Since we give each defender a name, we also name the seven defensive pass areas. This helps us make reference to the specific areas we want our defenders to cover. The frontside is to the direction of the coverage call or to the formation side (*Diagram 9-1*).

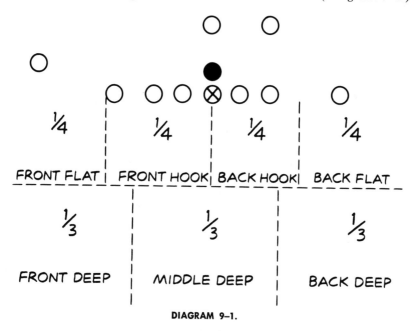

DIAGRAM 9-1.

While we often tell our defenders to sprint to the middle of their zone and play the ball, our coaching point is to play the deepest receiver in his zone. If only one receiver enters his zone, we want the secondary defender to play as close to the potential receiver as possible, but never to run out of his zone. We want the defender as near to the receiver as possible in order to be closer to the receiver once the ball has been thrown.

Cover One

Coverage one is called when the safety man is able to rotate in only one direction. This means he is able to cover the front side deep one-third zone and pick up the potential receiver in that area.

In *Diagram 9-2* the outside linebackers drop off on a forty-five degree angle and pick up the outside flat zones. These linebackers

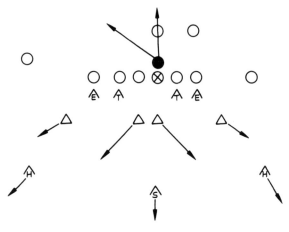

DIAGRAM 9–2. Cover One

should keep their bodies low and sprint back to their assigned areas keeping their eyes on the passes over their inside shoulder. We teach our linebackers to look through the receivers sprinting back to their flat depth of about ten yards, ready to cover any defender who may break into their assigned zone.

The inside linebackers are taught to get back to their hook zones as quickly as possible. Their routes should gain width and depth while checking for any receivers to make an inside cut into their areas. A quick glance back at the passer will indicate any necessary adjustment in their rotating paths. Once the passer sets up, we want our inside linebacker's shoulders squared to the line of scrimmage at a depth of twelve yards. Once the linebackers gain their maximum depth, they should be under control ready to break in any direction to intercept the pass.

Once the play is recognized as a pass, the defensive halfbacks should sprint back to their respective zones under control. The defender's path depends upon field position. If the halfback is into the short side of the field, he will take a deeper angle so he will be able to get deeper if the ball is passed into his area of responsibility.

The safety man retreats to his area under control and has a panoramic view of the entire pass pattern. The speed of our safety depends upon the speed of the offensive receivers. All of our deep secondary receivers are taught to go directly to the ball once it has been put into the air and make the defensive play whether it be attacking the ball or blocking the first potential receiver. All of these defenders must

continually work on their proper defensive cushion on the deepest
receiver in their particular zones.

Cover one is called and the halfback to the flanker's side yells,
"Deep middle" to the outside linebacker. This reminds the linebacker
to take over the deep middle responsibility if the quarterback sprints
away from the flanker (*Diagram 9-3*). The linebacker must sprint

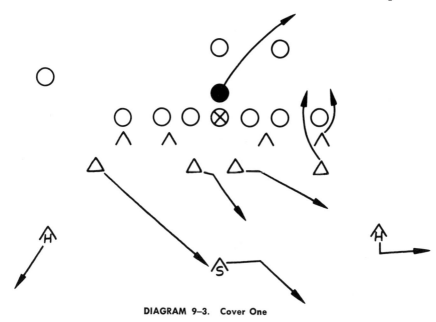

DIAGRAM 9–3. Cover One

back on a forty-five degree angle gaining as much depth as possible.
The backside halfback covers the deep back one-third zone looking
for the flanker to run a flag or up pattern. The middle safety man now
follows his defensive rule covering the deep outside one-third. The
front one-fourth flat zone is covered by the right defensive halfback.
The defensive halfback begins to drop back but levels off once the flow
comes his way and covers the outside quarter of the field. The frontside defensive halfback's coverage releases the outside linebacker
enabling him to blitz the offensive flow. This puts added pressure on
the passer forcing him to throw quickly and often off balance, which
helps the defense to intercept these off target passes. The left inside
linebacker begins his lateral movement, then begins to drop back directly over the center, as the quarterback continues on his sprint-out
course. The depth of his path depends upon the time the passer takes
to throw the ball. While the right inside linebacker begins to move
laterally he then drops back to cover the frontside hook zone.

Cover Two

Cover two is used against a primarily sprint-out quarterback whose strategy is to attack our perimeter containment.

Coverage two is designed to place a defender in the front quarter flat plus attack the sprint-out with a force-contain linebacker. The halfback defender away from the sprint-out is assigned to cover the deep two-thirds area. Coverage two means that the safety man can revolve two ways. This means he can cover the deep outside one-third to both sides of the field.

If the opposition uses the straight drop-back pass, the defensive coverage pattern is the same as cover one against the drop-back pass. Four of the linebackers are assigned to cover the four quarter hook and flat zones, while the secondary defenders are assigned to protect the thirds of the deep passing zones (*Diagram 9-4*).

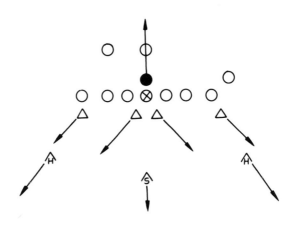

DIAGRAM 9–4. Cover Two

Whenever the quarterback sprints out against the two calls, our secondary defenders react in the manner illustrated in *Diagram 9-5*.

The halfback away from sprint-out should sprint to the middle of his zone, which is the deep two-thirds of the field. As the left defensive halfback sprints to his area, we want him to be looking for the throw-back pass. We teach him how to re-revolve if the passer uses the trans-continental pass. The defender's depth, plus the time it takes the passer

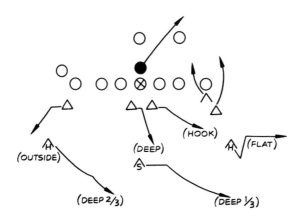

DIAGRAM 9–5. Cover Two

to sprint out and throw back, gives our defense ample time to react to the pass and get into the correct position to intercept the pass (*Diagram 9-5*).

The safety man covers the front deep one-third looking for the offensive left end to run a flag cut or some other deep route into the deep outside one-third area.

Once the play comes our right defensive halfback's way, he levels off his course and covers the deepest receiver in his flat quarter zone.

The outside linebacker attacks the quarterback's action while our inside right linebacker's zone is the right hook zone. The left inside linebacker slides over toward the middle, dropping back vertically as the quarterback continues his sprint-out course. The left outside linebacker looks for the throw-back or the reverse play coming back into his area. His retreating course is slower and more cautious than his defensive teammates because of the late threat of counter action into his area (*Diagram 9-5*).

Diagram 9-6 is similar to *Diagram 9-5,* only the quarterback sprints out to the defense's left and the defenders exchange their assignments because of the flow.

In coverage two, the defensive safety man can revolve left or right depending upon the flow of his quarterback key. If the quarterback drops straight back into a pocket, our safety man drops straight back to the deep middle third if cover two was called. Our quarterback does not revolve until the offensive quarterback breaks the imaginary guard's box. Once the quarterback sprints out across the plane, our safety revolves in the sprint-out direction (*Diagram 9-7*).

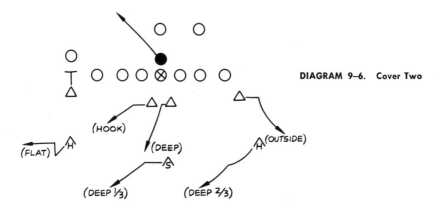

DIAGRAM 9–6. Cover Two

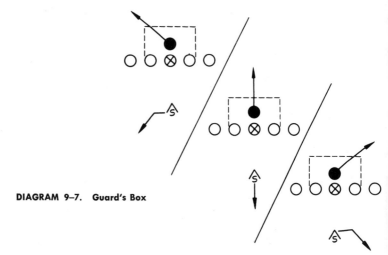

DIAGRAM 9–7. Guard's Box

Defending the Deep Two-Thirds of the Field

Playing a zone pass defense, the defender is taught to sprint to the middle of his zone and play the ball. The defender must be as wide as the widest and as deep as the deepest receiver in his zone. If he is assigned to cover the deep two-thirds of the field away from the quarterback's flow, he must get depth, vertically, as soon as possible. The deep defenders must attack the ball and drive through the receiver's head making a bona fide attempt to intercept the ball.

The deep two-thirds defender must gain depth because of the

threat of the long throw-back or transcontinental pass. The deep defender who is assigned the deep two-thirds responsibility must assume a safety man's duty. The depth factor is of paramount importance because of the defender's inside-out coverage assignment. As the flow goes away from the two-thirds defender always thinks throw-back pass.

The field position helps to determine the route and depth of the two-thirds defender. If the ball is in the middle of the field or the wide side is to the same defender's side, the route of retreat is on a forty-five degree angle. If the two-thirds defender is defending the short side of the field and a pass has been determined, the pass defender should drop straight back into his zone, if the quarterback drops straight back into his pocket, or if flow shows toward the defender. The straight vertical route is coached since the width of your zone has been narrowed to the short side of the field.

The halfback away from the quarterback's flow is taught to sprint back to the outside and then sprint to the inside, gaining depth and keeping the receiver or receivers inside of him. The most important prerequisite to making the defensive secondary play is to keep a good cushion on the receiver (*Diagrams 9–5* and *9–6*).

Cover Three

If the opposition uses a pro formation, or any other formation that employs two wide receivers, we use a cover three pass defense (*Diagram 9–8*).

Whenever cover three is called, our deep three defenders are locked into their three deep one-third zones and will never rotate or revolve out of this coverage. This defense is used primarily when we expect the opposition to pass. It is also used as our victory or prevent defense late in the game or just prior to the half when we expect the opposition to go for the long bomb.

Our defensive quarterback also calls this solid three deep defense whenever it is apparent that the safety man cannot cover the wide potential receivers in the deep outside one-third zones. As a change-up secondary call, we may use a three call instead of a one call if the formation shows a flankerback to one side and no split end on the other side.

All seven pass defenders must be constantly reminded that they

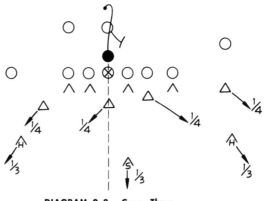

DIAGRAM 9–8. Cover Three

cover their respective zones, as illustrated in *Diagram 9–8*, regardless of whether the quarterback drops straight back or flows to his right or left. This is the most simplified cover to teach to pass defenders. But because of its simplicity, there always seems to be one or two defenders, in the early part of the season, who attempt to employ their own extemporaneous coverage technique to this pass defense. Therefore, we remind our pass defenders that this is a team pass defense and one individual move contrary to our preconceived plan could easily result in a "cheap" touchdown for the opposition.

These three defensive coverage patterns afford our defense a similar alignment "look," but vary our coverage patterns in an attempt to confuse the opposition's passing strategy.

With the ball on the hash mark, the deep safety man lines up over the offensive guard to the wide side of the field. This gives our middle secondary defender more of a chance to get to the true middle of the field. Since the ball is on the near hash mark, the true middle of our safety's zone is shaded toward the wide side of the field. All of our zones change slightly with field position and the sprint-out direction stretches toward the quarterback's flow.

Man-to-Man Call

By adjusting our safety man just prior to the snap of the ball and assigning our halfbacks and two linebackers' men, we can use a man-to-man defense with an eight man defensive front (*Diagram 9–9*).

The man-to-man defense is an excellent change-up from the regular zone defense of the three coverage calls previously discussed in this chapter. We like to use the man-to-man defense against the offense when they employ two wide receivers to both sides of their formation. We also use the man-to-man defense against the double wing formations and as a change of pace against any formation. The man-to-man

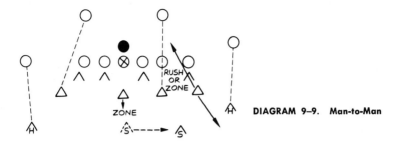

DIAGRAM 9–9.   Man-to-Man

coverage is a very flexible defense and can be used against any and all formations. Along with the straight man-to-man defense, we also use zone principles of inside-outside coverage. This means that we may be covering man-to-man on one side of our secondary defense and an isolated zone on the other side of the defense.

When using a man-to-man defense, we may free a defender to help double cover or help put the rush on the passes. All of our man-to-man assignments are clearly assigned and leave few doubts as to the defender's responsibility. Man-to-man defense assures the defense of not wasting a defender in an isolated zone where there is no receiver. Man-to-man teaching fundamentals help the defenders become better zone pass defenders because they learn to play closer to the man in their assigned zone. The selection of their intended receiver also helps to relieve the defender of any question as to his keys or responsibility once the ball has been put into play, and split second timing and reactions are the difference between an interception or a touchdown pass. Preplay man-to-man assignments also put our best defenders against their best receivers and help to eliminate the offensive strategy of isolating our weakest defender play after pass play. Playing man-to-man defense has helped to teach our pass defenders to be more aggressive when attacking the ball. The man-to-man competition helps bring out the best combative instincts of the defenders who finally understand the necessity of going through the man for the ball. It also teaches the defender to search the potential receiver by bringing both arms and hands down over the opponent's shoulders in an attempt to straighten out the receiver's arms, thus causing the opponent to drop the pass.

Regardless of whether we are playing man-to-man or zone, we always coach all of our pass defenders to sprint to the ball once it has been thrown. This is necessary because once the ball is in the air, the defender forgets his man or zone and thinks only of getting to the ball as soon as possible to make the interception.

With well-coached pass blocking, professional-like pass patterns, and the accuracy of today's passers, we feel that the defensive secondaries must use some form of man-to-man pass defense.

The Three Deep 44

10

The 44 three deep pass defense has an advantage over other pass defenses because it has the ability to shoot a linebacker on sprint-out passes, while still covering the defensive pass zone. This same defense is easily adaptable to man-to-man pass coverage because it can easily shift one or more linebackers to play one or more eligible receivers on a man-to-man basis.

Rotation Pass Defense

Using the 44 Rotation pass defense, two linebackers cover the short hook zones versus the sprint-out pass. The frontside inside linebacker forces the passer with the intent of tackling the passer or forcing the quarterback to rush his pass. The frontside outside linebacker chugs the defensive tight end and then goes after the passer from an inside-out angle on his delayed rush. The front or playside outside safety comes up and plays the flat zone toward the sprint-out, while the middle safety man revolves to cover the playside's deep one-third zone. The right safety man revolves toward the sprint-out passer and is assigned to defend the deep two-thirds zone (*Diagram 10-1*).

Combination Pass Defense (Zone and Man-to-Man)

If the sprint-out pass is directed toward a split end, the 44 defense will assign an individual deep defender to cover the split man. The outside linebacker plays the near side running back man-to-man in the event he takes off on a flare or flat course (*Diagram 10-2*).

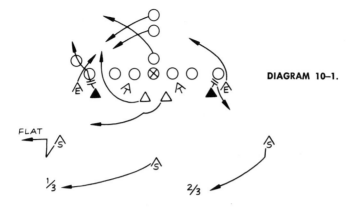

DIAGRAM 10–1.

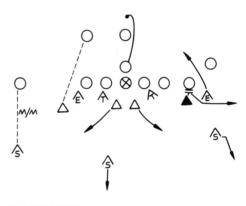

DIAGRAM 10–2.

Straight Three Deep Zone Pass Defense

The straight three deep zone defense is also used with all three of the deep defenders covering their deep zones. This is a nonrevolving defense regardless of whether the passer sprints out in either direction or just drops straight back into his pocket. Both of the defensive ends use their outside-in rushing techniques with the outside linebackers assigned to cover the flats after chugging the tight ends. Both of the inside linebackers cover their hook zones on all sprint-out and drop-back passes (*Diagram 10–3*).

The three deep zone pass coverage is basically the same against the pro formation. But if the 44 defense calls for tight double coverage

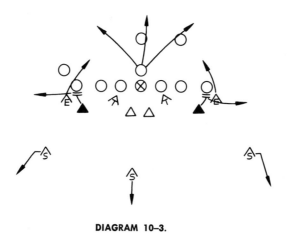

DIAGRAM 10–3.

on both wide defenders, the outside linebacker to the tight end side will move out to a head-up position on the flanker. But since there is no immediate threat of a quick hitter (no one in the halfback's position), the 44 defense can be sound in this alignment against both the passing and the running game (*Diagram 10-4*).

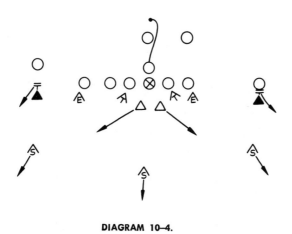

DIAGRAM 10–4.

Man-to-Man Pass Defense

Using the three deep (locked-in) zone defense is weakest against the in-between passes. These are the hooks, curls, circles, and crossing pass patterns that attack the gray area between the linebackers and the deep secondary zones. Therefore, to limit the completions in this zone, some type of a man-to-man pass defense must be incorporated with these zone principles.

All of the man-to-man pass defenders must be taught to take away the potential pass receiver's favorite move. This is why each defender must be taught to line up properly and take away the inside or the outside pass route. On short passes, the defenders must play the receiver as tight as possible all the way and play the deeper receivers looser until the ball is in the air.

All of the pass defenders must recognize their assigned man to key. Along with the proper keys, each defender must take his proper alignment and depth depending upon the defensive football strategy of the play.

Diagram 10–5 illustrates the outside left linebacker picking up the

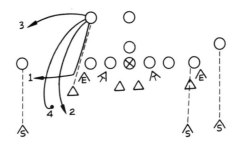

DIAGRAM 10–5.

right halfback on a man-to-man assignment. The usual pass patterns for the halfbacks are (1) flat, (2) circle, (3) flare, or (4) hook. Therefore, the linebacker's alignment should be to the halfback's outside so he can take away the near back's favorite cuts. If the halfback blocks, the linebacker should drop off ready to cover the flat or the curl area against the split end's cut.

Diagram 10-6 also moves the middle safety man toward the side of the offensive formation's two quick receivers. Now both of the outside linebackers are assigned to play the two split running backs man to man. The outside right linebacker still has time to chug and delay the tight end if his near halfback takes off in his direction.

In *Diagram 10-7* the middle safety man draws the offensive slot man for his assignment. The outside safeties cover the outside offensive

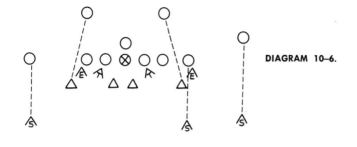

DIAGRAM 10–6.

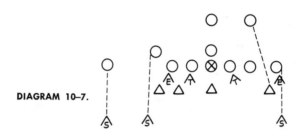

DIAGRAM 10–7.

player man-to-man. This may signal the two left linebackers and the inside right linebacker to slide over toward the slot if the formation is to the wide side of the field. This would give the right side of the defense a 61 look, while the left side would take on a 62 alignment. Whenever we rotate toward the split end's side, the defensive tackle may choose to level off his stance parallel to the line of scrimmage or may stay in his regular angular 44 stance.

The left outside linebacker does not chug the right end unless the offensive right halfback blocks or runs away from the right end's position (*Diagram 10–8*). The right and middle safety men may use

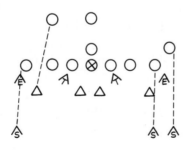

DIAGRAM 10–8.

their inside-outside secondary call against the offensive left end and
wingback.

Motion Adjustments

The four linebacker defense has an advantage over other defenses
because the linebackers adjust to motion, while still keeping the consistent three deep secondary.

One of the inside middle linebackers is designated as captain and
he makes the motion call. The motion call is either "Motion Right" or
"Motion Left." Motion is called as soon as the back begins to move to
enable the three linebackers to make their adjustments as quickly as
possible. In *Diagram 10-9* the wingback's motion puts us in the same

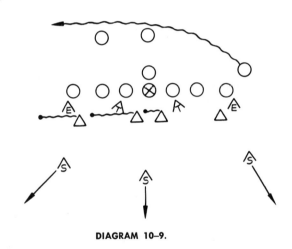

DIAGRAM 10–9.

62-61 alignment in our defensive line as we used against the wide slot
in *Diagram 10-7*. The pass coverage zones for the 44 linebackers are
the flat zone for the left outside linebacker, the left hook zone for
the left inside linebacker, the middle hook zone for the right inside
linebacker, and the right hook or curl zone for the right outside linebacker. The three deep safeties cover their deep one-third zones regardless of motions, although the left safety man may adjust his
alignment slightly to the outside.

If the opposition uses the slot formation and runs the slot man in
motion, the 44 defense will cover this offensive maneuver in two ways.
When the defense is playing man-to-man coverage with its linebackers, the linebacker assigned to the slot man will follow him all
the way. This means the left outside linebacker in *Diagram 10-10*

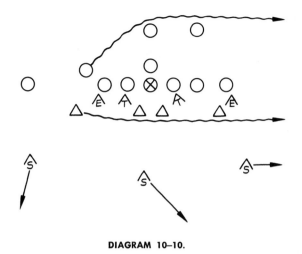

DIAGRAM 10–10.

covers the man in motion prior to the snap of the ball, but also shadows the slot man until the play ends. The outside right safety man may also adjust his alignment slightly wider as the motion man widens. But all of the three defenders are still playing their regular three deep zones.

Another way of playing the slot man is to shift from a 61 "look" to a Split 6 "look" as soon as the slot man goes into motion (*Diagram 10–11*). The 61 alignment allows the 44 defense to place a linebacker

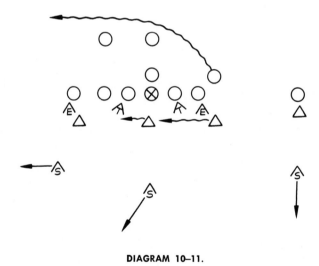

DIAGRAM 10–11.

on the split end's nose and only adjusts two linebackers to move back to the Split 6 type of defense. Both of these adjustments would be based upon the previous week's scouting report and would be practiced for the entire week. These two different ways of reacting to motion hinder the offensive quarterback's strategy because he never knows, for certain, what exact defense the opponent will play his motion call. Now the defense has forced the offense into playing a guessing game.

Along with jamming the ends, playing zone pass defense, and then shifting to Man-to-Man pass defense, the 44 defense also depends upon a strong blitzing attack to keep the offensive passing attack honest. One of the favorite 44 blitzes is to barrel both inside linebackers into the center-guard gaps and step the tackles around into the guard-tackle gaps (*Diagram 10–12*).

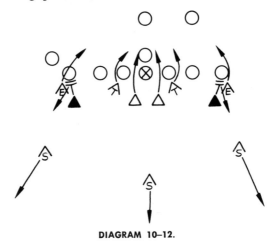

DIAGRAM 10–12.

The barrel can also be changed on one side by crossing the inside linebacker into the guard-tackle gap and pinching the tackle into the center-guard gap (*Diagram 10–13*).

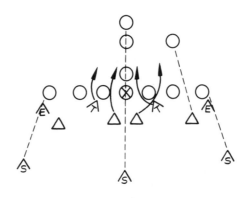

DIAGRAM 10–13.

The two inside linebackers also exchange blitz assignments by crossing and blitzing into the opposite center-guard gap (*Diagram 10-14*).

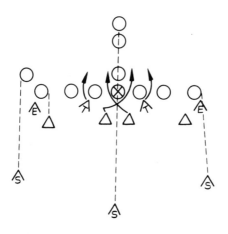

DIAGRAM 10-14.

Diagrams 10-12, 10-13, and *10-14* are all good blitzes versus the straight drop-back passes, but against the sprint- or roll-out variety, the 44 defense often uses two blitzes. One may come from the outside and the other from the inside. The shooting linebackers' moves help to free the defensive tackles and ends. In *Diagram 10-15* the left

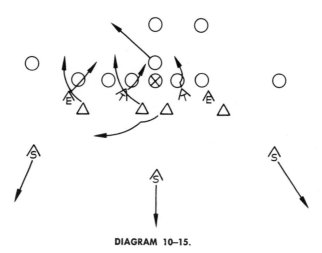

DIAGRAM 10-15.

defensive tackle and inside left linebacker use a cross charge, while the left end pinches inside on a force maneuver and the left outside linebacker loops outside into the left defensive end's position.

Whenever the quarterback has a habit of sprinting out to the split end's side, the 44 defense often calls for an inside rush by both linebackers to the split end's side. *Diagram 10–16* shows a gap stack in the center-guard gap to the split end's side, with the defensive tackle driving into the center's outside shoulder and the stacked linebacker shooting into the gap. The outside right stack also sends the stacked outside right linebacker into the guard-tackle gap with the defensive right end containing the sprint-out play.

DIAGRAM 10–16.

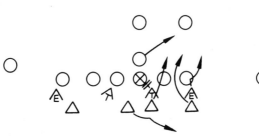

Pro 43
Defensive Methods
and Techniques
vs. Pro Formations

11

Pass defense today is not just three or four secondary defenders playing man-to-man or zone pass coverage, but rather, it is an eleven man team effort. Many college passing attacks today have reached the heights that the professional football teams reached ten years ago. Many high school football passing programs are also on a par with the college passing attacks of a decade ago. Today's passer is bigger, has a stronger passing arm, and is better coached than ever before. The pass receivers' patterns are becoming more complicated and scientific each season. Pragmatically speaking, the improvement of the passing game has forced the defensive coordinators into using a multiple series of blitzing, zone, man-to-man, and combination defensive pass coverage techniques to combat the emphasis being placed on the pass.

Each year it seems that we are facing more wide pro offenses, and thus we have adopted the 43 pro defense to contain the wide open passing game.

There are times we are forced to inject a fifth back in a definite passing situation, thus actually making our pass defense a 4-2-5 defense in reality. Since the offensive attack is equipped with hundreds of offensive variations, the defense must also use several variations to attack each offensive formation to keep the signal caller guessing. Defensively we never want the offense to dictate a one way method of defensing a particular pass, or they may be able to "throw" us out of the ball game.

The following discussion and diagrams are some of the defensive stunts and pass defensive techniques we have used in conjunction with our pro defense versus the wide open pro formations.

Against the pro passing offense, we use our basic 43 defense (*Diagram 11-1*). Terminology is important to our staff for correct

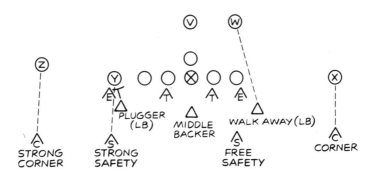

DIAGRAM 11-1. Basic 43 Man-to-Man vs. Pro

identification because of our many defensive adjustments. Both of our ends and tackles are of course labelled (E and T) respectively. We name our linebackers according to their assignments or alignments. The linebacker to the strong or tight end's side is referred to as our (P) or Plugger because it is up to this backer to plug up the off tackle hole and to plug or hold up the tight end on a passing down. Our (M) or middle linebacker's alignment is to defend the middle of our defense against the fullback trap, middle screen, and the center field hook zone. The Walker linebacker is referred to as (W) because he is often in a walk-away type position and has the responsibility to stop the remaining halfback's swing or flat pass patterns, as well as the look and curl in patterns by the split end.

The cornerbacks are identified as (C) as in previous chapters. Our safety men line up according to the strong and weak side of the offense. The strong safety man (S) usually lines up to the formation's power or tight end and flanker's side, while our free safety man may line up on the split end's side; in case of a pass, he is free to cover in any direction he chooses. We have drawn a dotted line from each potential receiver to a specific defender. The letters M/M symbolize Man-to-Man Coverage. The offensive man represents the individual keys on a pass for our pass defenders. The only pass defender who does not have a specific man to key is our free safety, and as stated previously, he is free to roam on any pass play. The dotted lines also represent the defender's man-to-man assignment whenever our secondary captain calls for man-to-man coverage. These man-to-man coverage assignments are kept regardless of whether the quarterback drops back into his pocket or sprints out to either side.

Therefore, in *Diagram 11–1* we can have a four man rush with a free safety man to roam, our middle linebacker covers the middle hook zone, and our Plugger or left linebacker holds up the tight end or covers the left flat zone. We could change up on our previously mentioned man-to-man coverage by blitzing our three linebackers.

"Zone pass coverage" may also be used against this offensive formation from the same defensive alignment, as illustrated in *Diagram 11–2*.

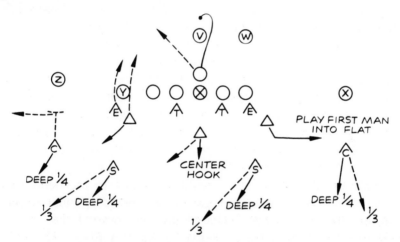

FOUR DEEP ZONE COVERAGE vs. POCKET = ⟶
THREE DEEP ZONE COVERAGE vs. SPRINT OUT LEFT = – – – – ►

DIAGRAM 11–2.

We use a four deep zone coverage secondary against the wide pro offensive set with a straight back pocket pass by the quarterback. All of our four deep defenders cover their zones depending upon field position, direction of the quarterback's path, combined with the routes of the offensive pass receivers. The left corner covers the deep left outside zone while our right corner sprints to the deep right outside area. Our right safety man is assigned the deep middle zone while our strong side safety man has a special zone assignment which takes away the seam between our left cornerback and our right safety man's zones. If no one attempts to split the seam, we have our strong side safety man take away the best cut by either the tight end or the flanker depending upon the pattern we expect on a given down playing the percentage pattern, according to previous scouting points and opponent's game films.

Along with our four deep zone coverage, we have our three linebackers cover their three hook or flat zones. The Plugger covers the tight end's potential hook zone and may then check the outside left defensive flat if either the tight end or flanker's pattern is directed in that open area (*Diagram 11-2*).

If the quarterback sprints out toward the defense's left, the left corner covers the flat to his side, and the left safety, right safety, and right corner cover their deep thirds respectively (*Diagram 11-2*).

When the quarterback should sprint out to the defense's left (dotted line), either or both the defensive left end and left linebackers attack the sprinting-out passer (*Diagram 11-2*). If the defensive end shoots his inside gap, then the left linebacker loops outside of the offensive end's original position. Our middle linebacker drops back and on an angle toward the quarterback's sprint-out direction. As he sprints, we want him to look for the offensive tight end. If the tight end hooks, we expect our middle linebacker to cover him. If the tight end attempts to cross our middle linebacker's face, we want our defender to knock him down before the ball is in the air.

Whenever the quarterback should sprint out to the defender's right, the secondary defenders revolve as soon as the defender sprints out beyond the guard's box. (Dotted line just beyond the outside shoulders of both the offensive guards.) (*Diagram 11-3*) The right backer assignment calls for him to force-contain the quarterback sprinting out in his direction. We may alter our linebacker's course if we find that the quarterback is of little threat as a runner. This alteration would also change the assignment of our free safety because we would not want both the free safety man and the Walker in the same flat area.

Our right safety man covers the flat in an invert type of assignment, while our cornerback covers the deep right outside zone. The strong safety takes the deep middle zone, while the left corner man drops back into the deep left outside zone. The left linebacker drops

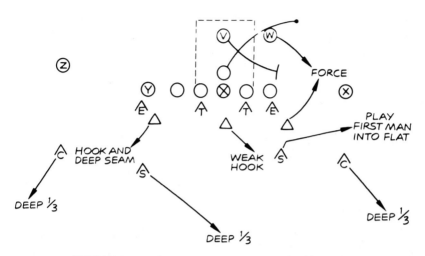

DIAGRAM 11-3. Three Deep Zone with Change (Semi Invert)

back into the defensive seam caused by the quick revolving secondary quartet. The middle linebacker's assignment is the middle hook zone which moves as the quarterback moves toward the defender's right.

Another way of playing the wide pro formation is to place our left backer directly over the tight end and hit him by delivering a blow holding up the tight end (*Diagram 11-4*). Once the tight end releases, we coach the linebacker to play this intended receiver. If the tight end hooks, we want our backer to take away the hook by playing in front of the receiver. If the tight end breaks outside, the linebacker should

DIAGRAM 11-4. Three Deep Zones with Inside Corner Pressure

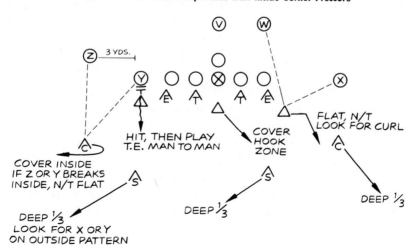

look for the delayed pattern or the split end's curl route. The left defensive end is still responsible for a contained rush on the pocket passer, even though the end is now inside his regular end position. The left corner man keys both the Y and Z receivers (flanker and tight end) and covers either defender if any one of them makes an inside cut. Our left safety plays the deep outside one-third, while the right safety man's assignment is to cover the deep middle one-third, while our right corner covers the other outside one-third. The right linebacker starts for the flat, but if no one shows, he takes a forty-five degree angle looking for the split end to run the curl cut. The middle linebacker is assigned to cover the weak side hook zone.

Diagram 11–4 is another method of defending against the pass while in much the same defensive alignment as in *Diagram 11–3.* The only change over the previous defensive alignments is that we moved the left linebacker out and moved the defensive end into the left backer's former position on the outside shoulder of the offensive right tackle. The linebacker's role is to hit and hold up the tight end, then drop back and play him man-to-man. If the tight end hooks, we expect the linebacker to take away the inside hook zone; and if the end breaks to the outside flat, we want our backer sprinting with him to the outside.

Since the offense has moved the flanker slightly to the inside, we change the left corner's assignment to key both the flankerback and the tight end. If either key tries to cut to their inside, we assign the corner man to play either receiver tight to the inside. The second part of our left corner man's assignment is to cover the flat zone if Z or Y do not break inside. Our strong safety man takes the deep outside zone to the strong side and looks for either Z or Y on an outside pass pattern. The cornerback covers the deep right one-third area, while our right cornerback keys both W and X (halfback and split end) as he sprints to pressure either receiver in the flat area. If these two potential receivers do not make a flat cut, the corner changes his flat course to a forty-five degree angle toward the flag and looks for the curl pattern or anyone crossing his face. The middle linebacker drops back and covers the weak side hook zone.

Whenever our team faces an outstanding receiver, we adjust our defensive secondary so that we can take away the opponent's favorite receiver and his best pass pattern. If this top receiver happens to be the opposition's split end, we set up our defensive strategy to double team this receiver. We would assign our right safety man and right cornerback to pressure the split end, assigning the right safety man to take away the inside area and the corner defender to attack the receiver from the rear.

In *Diagram 11–5* we have illustrated the split end making an in-

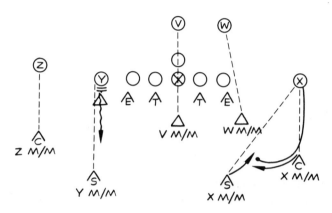

DIAGRAM 11–5.   43 Defense and Double Teamming the Split End

side curl cut with both our right safety man and right corner covering the outside receiver man to man. With these two defenders sandwiching the receiver, we are trying to take away the pass from their favorite receiver through our defensive secondary double coverage technique. Our other defenders use their respective keys and play man-to-man coverage.

We can use the double coverage technique against any one of the opposition's potential receivers. The defense does not always have to be in man-to-man coverage because we can also have double coverage within the defensive zone pattern. The way we would double cover the split end is by double covering him with both our right linebacker and our right safety.

Double Covering the Pro Formation (Diagram 11–6)

On definite passing plays, our defensive strategy calls for doubling up on all four of the opponent's favorite receivers. We accomplish this defensive plan by lining up our four linebackers over these receivers and playing our linebackers man-to-man on the man over them. The three deep defenders are assigned their three deep zones. If any one of these receivers runs deep into one of these three deep zones, then

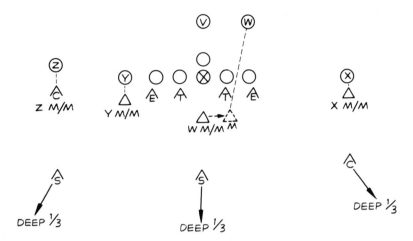

DIAGRAM 11–6.   Double Coverage on Four Quick Receivers

he will be double teamed by the linebacker or corner man who is playing him man-to-man and by the secondary receiver in the deep zone (*Diagram 11–6*).

We teach our two linebackers, our left linebacker and middle linebacker, to play their assigned keys man to man but to drop back and take away the short post cut if their keys block. If the two outside double cover men key block, we want them to drop back and cover their outside flats.

Another plan to double cover the two outside receivers using man-to-man coverage is to use a similar alignment as shown in *Diagram 11–6*. In this case, however, we would move the free safety over to key the tight end receiver man to man with the left linebacker still holding up the tight end. The middle linebacker continues to key the left halfback man to man. Therefore, we would have the right backer and right corner playing the split receiver man-to-man using the double teaming defensive technique. On the other side, both our left corner and strong left safety man will play the flanker receiver using their double teaming man-to-man defensive techniques.

Pass Defense vs. Double Strong Pro Formation

Organizing our defensive plan against the Double Strong Pro Formation, we used a combination of inside-outside, zone, and individual man-to-man coverage to cope with this wide strong formation (*Diagram 11–7*).

The most important facet of our combination coverage in *Dia-*

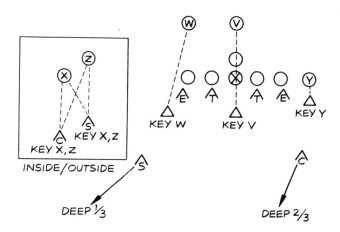

DIAGRAM 11-7. Combination Pass Defense vs. The Double Strong Pro

gram 11–7 is illustrated in the box on the left of the figure. The inside-outside coverage of our corner and free safety is a combination of a man-to-man defense within a zone area. These two players are given specific assignments for their inside (free safety) and outside (corner back) defensive secondary play. These are:

Drop-Back (Pocket Pass)

Inside (Safety man):

1. Two receivers release—Cover the inside receiver.
2. Two receivers release both inside—Cover deepest receiver.
3. Two receivers release both outside—Cover deepest receiver.
4. One receiver releases—You are free defender.

Outside (Corner man):

1. Two receivers release—Cover the outside receiver.
2. Two receivers release both inside—Cover the shortest receiver.
3. Two receivers release both outside—Cover the shortest receiver.
4. One receiver release—Cover receiver.

Backfield Flow To

Inside (Safety man):

    1. One receiver—Cover receiver.

Outside (Corner man):

    1. One receiver—Free, you may force or free lance.

Backfield Flow Away

Inside (Safety man):

    1. One receiver—Free, you may force or free lance.

Outside (Corner man):

    1. One receiver—Cover receiver.

The reasoning behind these rules is that we want to keep our defenders from getting picked off or screened out by the two close opponent's receivers. If both of the receivers would cross their routes according to the rules, our defenders would just play their zones and would not get involved in switching assignments physically or make any mental mistakes by using an incorrect oral call.

Our other three linebackers (left, right, and middle) all play their man individually man-to-man. If any one of these offensive players block, the defender who is keying him is free to play the ball.

The three deep zones are covered by the two defensive deep backs. The strong safety is responsible for the deep left outside one-third zone, while our sprinter is responsible for the remaining two-thirds of deep area.

This offense is used to take advantage of three outstanding receivers. The two wide receivers had many individual patterns to take advantage of the perimeter defensive secondary coverage. It also tries to isolate the strong, outstanding tight end on a one on one isolated coverage pattern. But our combination secondary coverage illustrated in *Diagram 11-7* forces the deep defender to be covered on a two on one defensive technique. Therefore, we feel the odds are on our side whenever the passer attempts to throw deep against our Combination Pass Defense.

Pass Defense vs. the Strong Pro Formations

We use several methods to attack the overloaded strong pro formations so that the offense will not limit our attacking power. One method is to use a combination coverage on the two wide receivers if they are into the short side of the field.

The strong pro formation places three receivers on the overloaded or strong side of the formation. Therefore, we change our secondary alignment and their keys so that we can meet power with power (*Diagram 11-8*). We line up our free safety man over the

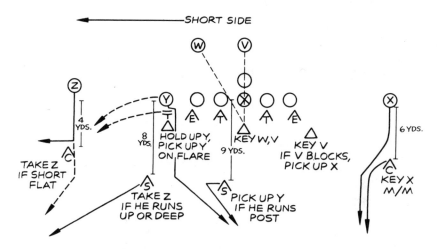

DIAGRAM 11-8.   Man-to-Man and Zone vs. Strong Pro

strong side guard's nose about nine yards deep and instruct him to key and pick up the tight end if he runs a post or any deep inside cuts. Our strong side safety man lines up splitting the difference between the tight end and flanker about eight yards deep. The actual depth of the strong safety depends upon the down, field position, speed of the potential receivers, our safety's own speed, etc. His defensive pass assignment is to take away the flanker's deep pattern. He is cautioned to be ready to help on the flanker's sideline and up cut. The left corner's assignment is to defend against the flanker man's short cut. The defensive corner man's alignment is over a slightly outside leverage on the flankerback and approximately four yards deep depending upon the width of the flankerback's split. The far side safety man plays the split end man-to-man at a depth of six yards. We teach our defenders always to play on the outside or inside shoulder of the defensive man they are playing man-to-man. The coaching point behind this theory is that we want our pass defender to take away one of the receiver's cuts. If the defender plays head-up on the receiver, he gives the receiver an unlimited number of routes to choose from. Conversely, the top receivers are always taught to run directly at the defensive back so that they are head-up on the defender to gain their optional number of cuts.

An alternate method of secondary coverage versus the strong pro offense is to play a strict zone defense in the secondary. Regardless of whether the quarterback drops back into the pocket or sprints out to either side, our secondary stays in the exact zone as drawn in *Diagram 11-9*. All of our defensive secondary defenders are locked in their

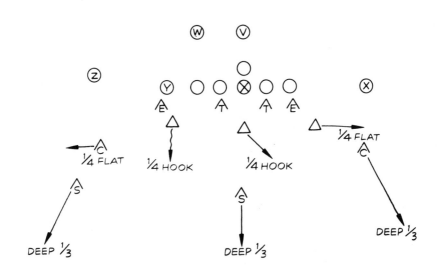

DIAGRAM 11-9.   Zone vs. Strong Pro

seven zone areas and this minimizes the chance of the defenders making a mistake due to a missed assignment. We like this coverage against the strong pro set because it is the easiest method to teach, and our players have confidence in this particular method of defending against this overloaded defense. All of our defenders are taught to drop back into their zones quickly and never to let a receiver get deeper than any defender in a given zone.

The drop-back zone move by our defenders is not a backward shuffle technique, but it is a sprint-back technique, turning the entire body (except for the head, which is watching the passer) toward the goal line. We coach our zone defenders that the only honest man on the football field is the passer and to adjust their sprint back paths depending upon the passer's direction. Once the passer throws the ball, we expect all defenders to go for the ball, intercepting the football at its highest point. We want all of our pass defenders to sprint through the receiver while going for the interception. Aggressiveness is an essential characteristic for all secondary defenders. All pass defenders must develop confidence for playing the ball. Our entire coaching staff emphasizes that we have the most solid and outstanding pass defense in the nation. We want all of our pass defenders to be on the attack whenever the opposition puts the ball into the air.

Free Coverage

We use free coverage whenever we want to use our three deep zone and assign our free safety man to man-to-man coverage or to key offensive flow. Free coverage is similar to basketball's four man box zone with a defensive chaser assigned to the opponent's leading scorer (*Diagram 11–10*). We place our free safety in one of five positions against the pro defense:

(1) Three yards away from the flanker on his inside keying him man to man. Occasionally we tell our free safety to chug the flanker back and then play him tight or fake a chug and play him tight all over the field. We use this coverage if the flanker is their top receiver and on a definite passing down. The double coverage by our free safety

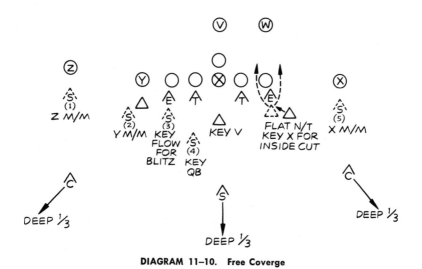

DIAGRAM 11–10. Free Coverge

helps to confuse the opposition with our regular double coverage when the left cornerback only plays the flanker in the short zone, letting the deep defender play him alone in the deep one-third outside zone. In this coverage, we tell our free safety to run with the flanker all the way down field as far as the receiver goes.

If a sweep shows the free safety's way, he does not come up until the ball carrier has crossed the line of scrimmage. He is keyed to the run by the oral call of our other defender.

(2) The two position is designated for our free safety to play the Y man in man-to-man coverage. If the tight end blocks in, we want our free safety man to make sure he is not "slow blocking" and to attack the ball carrier if flow comes his way. At times we may wish to blitz our free safety man outside or inside of the offensive tight end with the left linebacker first drawing the flanker's block, then dropping off into the flat. This cross charge helps to confuse the offensive blocking pattern and is most effective against the sprint-out teams who like to sprint to the strong side (*Diagram 11–11A*).

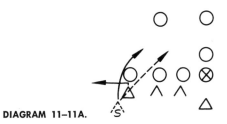

DIAGRAM 11–11A.

(3) This position is used primarily against the strong side running attack. The free safety is on his own and may attack the flow his way in any method he wishes. We also have set safety blitz stunts from this alignment.

(4) This is our basic free safety man's position against the pro formation. Our safety man keys the quarterback and plays the action by "ear." This means he can pick up a man in man-to-man coverage, attack the run, or play a particular zone. His play resembles a center fielder, and he can play any pass he can get his hands on. In reality this rover man gives us a 44 defense. This type of a defense is strongest against the running game.

(5) The free safety plays the split end man-to-man. As soon as we assign our free safety to key the split end, we move our right linebacker in closer or possibly stacked over our defensive end. From these positions, we want our linebacker to rush the passer. We like to

PLAYER	ALIGNMENT	RUN ASSIGNMENT	PASS ASSIGNMENT
Left Cornerback and Right Cornerback	—3 Yards Wide —5 Yards Deep —As ball is snapped, sprint to deep outside	FLOW TO: Force play maintaining a 2 yard relationship with our end and force-contain the ball FLOW AWAY: Sprint to your ⅓. Go to revolve pattern.	Outside ⅓ Zone
Strong Safety	—7 Yards Deep —Over End —As ball is snapped, sprint to deep middle	Basically force with Inside-Outside Angle	Middle ⅓ Zone
Free Safety	—7 Yards Deep —Over Tackle; Depends upon key —Prior to snap of ball, move to position	Attack Ball Carrier	1. Assigned man or zone. 2. Outstanding receiver 3. Scouting or film tendencies.

DIAGRAM 11-11. Free Coverage

Coaching Points:

1. Used against outstanding receiver.
2. Free safety must sprint after he makes up his break and continue in the direction to attack the ball carrier or for an interception.
3. Offensive formation dictates free safety's alignment.
4. Film and scouting report tendencies will be our directive.
5. The free safety has five basic positions.

use our free man keying the split end against the sprint-out action toward the split end because now our linebacker can attack the sprint-out quarterback before he gets under way by blitzing the linebacker inside or outside the short side offensive tackle.

Diagram 11–11 explains our free coverage defensive secondary coverage. This chart explains the alignment, run assignment, and pass assignments for our cornerbacks, strong safety, and free safety man. All of these assignments are listed in a concise chart.

The five important coaching points for this formation are:

1. Use against the outstanding receiver.
2. Free safety must sprint after he makes up his break and continue in the direction to attack the ball carrier or for an interception.
3. Offensive formation dictates free safety's assignment.
4. Film and scouting report tendencies will be our directive.
5. The free safety has five basic positions.

Diagram 11–12 is a sister defensive secondary pattern to be used against the pro formation. In this diagram, however, we use a different alignment in our defensive front by shifting our left defensive tackle to a position over the center and move the middle linebacker over the right offensive guard. Therefore, we are strong against the running game to the two remaining backs' side.

We try to make our free safety appear to be playing man-to-man coverage by covering the flanker for the first five yards in man-to-man coverage. After that, the safety drops off into the flat. Our left linebacker also plays the tight end man-to-man if he veers inside. But if the tight end angles outside, the linebacker is assigned to cover the strong side hook zone. The middle linebacker remains in his man-to-man coverage on the fullback, while our right linebacker to the weak side cues the set halfback and picks him out if he flares or sprints into the flat. If the halfback blocks, we tell our right linebacker to pick up the split end and play in front of him. Therefore, if the halfback blocks, we may be able to sandwich the split end in between our linebacker and right cornerback. All three of our deep backs play their keys but cover the deep one-third zones on any type of pass action.

This defensive pattern resembles the regular five man Oklahoma Defense with the right linebacker in an almost walk-away position and the left safety man playing in the Oklahoma's corner or "true" monster position.

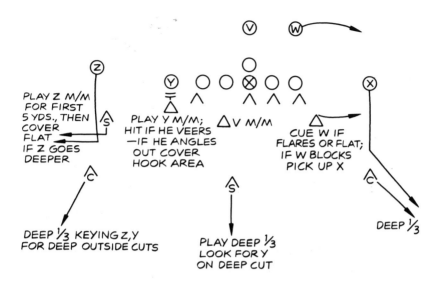

DIAGRAM 11-12. Deep Three Zone Backers Man-to-Man

The passing strategy behind the wide slot alignment is to stretch the defensive perimeter and secondary as wide as possible, and then try to hit the deep seams as well as run short quick pass routes. To cut down the wide receiver's pass receiving efficiency, we double cover the two wide ends and play a combination of a man-to-man and zone pass coverage technique against this wide formation.

We use a combination of a man-to-man and zone pass defense against the side slot formation in *Diagram 11-13.*

The Plugger chugs the Y receiver then drops into the flat on a forty-five degree angle to the inside to cover the flat. This inside angle will also take away the quick look-in pass. The middle linebacker key is the offensive fullback (V) and is responsible for protecting the opened defensive gap caused by the right defensive tackle's loop into the center-guard gap. Our right outside linebacker hits and holds up the X man, then checks the near back to his side for a wide flare route. The right linebacker drops back and takes away the split end's curl or sideline cut by sprinting back to a point between the passer and the X receiver. This position forces the passer to loft the ball over the linebacker's head. This slight delay helps to put the sprinter in perfect position to intercept the pass by playing the split end man to man.

The deep secondary defenders all play their assigned men using

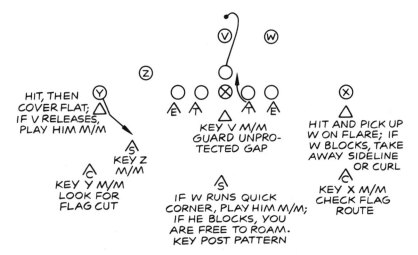

HIT, THEN
COVER FLAT;
IF V RELEASES,
PLAY HIM M/M

KEY Z
M/M

KEY Y M/M
LOOK FOR
FLAG CUT

KEY V M/M
GUARD UNPRO-
TECTED GAP

IF W RUNS QUICK
CORNER, PLAY HIM M/M;
IF HE BLOCKS, YOU
ARE FREE TO ROAM.
KEY POST PATTERN

HIT AND PICK UP
W ON FLARE; IF
W BLOCKS, TAKE
AWAY SIDELINE
OR CURL

KEY X M/M
CHECK FLAG
ROUTE

DIAGRAM 11–13. Man-to-Man and Zone vs. Wide Slot

man-to-man coverage. The left linebacker keys the Y receiver man to man looking for the flag or other deep cuts. The strong side safety man keys the slot man (Z) man to man and is free only if the Z man blocks. Our free safety keys the W offensive back and picks him up if he runs a quick deep corner cut. If the halfback blocks, the free safety is free to roam and play the ball. The right cornerback keys X man to man and is especially aware of the deep flag or sideline and go pass patterns.

Multiple Safety
Blitz Attack

12

                The safety blitz can be used from any num-
·ber of secondary alignments: The four deep, three deep, or corner
secondary looks. Probably the most effective secondary alignment to
spring the safety blitz from is the four deep or four across the board
deep alignment because any of the four defensive backs may be the
predetermined man to blitz. Once the defensive blitzer has made his
move, the secondary may utilize a zone or man-to-man defensive pass
coverage. If the box (corner or four deep) defense is used, the deep
defender may use a three man zone defense (*Diagram 12-1*), or with
the help of a linebacker, play a man-to-man pass defense (*Diagram
12-2*).

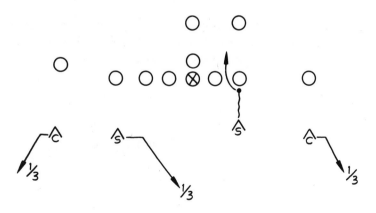

DIAGRAM 12–1. Safety Blitz to Zone

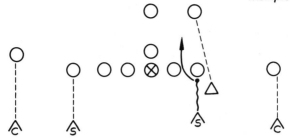

DIAGRAM 12-2. Saftey Blitz to Man-to-Man

If the defense is using a diamond (three deep alignment) and uses a safety blitz, they need help from a linebacker to cover the deep middle zone to continue in a three deep zone pass defense (*Diagram 12-3*).

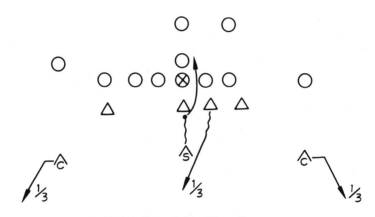

DIAGRAM 12-3. Safety Blitz to Zone

Whenever the defense employs a safety blitz from a three deep secondary and wants to use a man-to-man pass defense, two linebackers must key two eligible pass receivers. In *Diagram 12-4* the line-

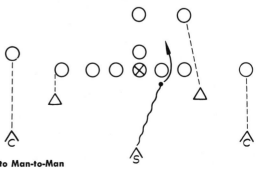

DIAGRAM 12-4. Safety Blitz to Man-to-Man

backers are assigned to cover the tight end and the halfback on the split end's side.

Along with the safety blitz, we like to blitz one or more linebackers to outnumber or at least eliminate two offensive blockers from doubling up on the defensive pass rushers. Against the threat of the sprint-out pass, we like to outnumber the blockers to the sprint outside using our safety blitz.

The safety blitz is not only a surprise weapon, but it also sends a quick, agile defender through the line to blitz the offensive attack. All of our defensive backs take great pride in stunting through the line because of the novelty of the blitz call. Tackling the passer for a sizeable loss is a crowd pleasing maneuver that delights our deep defenders. The safety blitz man is coached to make his body as small as possible to slide through the offensive line. Once he is through, he is taught to take the most direct route to the ball. We want the blitz man to fight through the blocker's head, but we also explain it is easier for a defensive back to feint out the blocker with a quick head or shoulder fake than it is to run over the blocker. All of our rushers are taught to hit and spin off the blockers along with their fakes.

If a pass play develops, we want the defender to tackle the passer high. We coach the defender to tackle the passer from the head down and never to leave his feet in an attempt to knock down the pass while rushing the passer. Once the rushing defender leaves his feet, the passer can outmaneuver the leaping defender. A successful safety blitz may not always result in tackling the passer for a loss, but he may put the pressure on the passer forcing him to rush his pass and throw off balance. These poorly timed passes often result in interceptions for the defense.

When a safety blitz is called, we coach the deep defender to edge up slowly toward the line of scrimmage just prior to the snap of the ball. Once he is close to the line of scrimmage, we actually ask him to hide behind one of the larger defensive linemen before he makes his break. Occasionally we ask a deep defender to fake his intentions to blitz and then return to his normal alignment and assignment just to keep the offensive signal caller honest.

The defensive safety blitz is not a one man stunt but is rather a team effort as the defensive linemen are assigned specific duties which help to open up a hole in the offensive blocking pattern. On certain stunts, our defensive linemen are assigned to stem or loop into offensive personnel to draw their blocks, while some of our linebackers are taught to blitz into other holes in the offensive line.

With third down and more than five yards to go and the opposition's offense outside of our twenty yard line, we may call for a safety blitz. If the opponent is primarily a sprint-out passing team and runs the sweep well, we will designate our safety blitz to attack the offensive end tackle gap to curtail the opposition's outside threat. *Diagram 12–5* illustrates the Safety "7" Blitz using a variety of defenses.

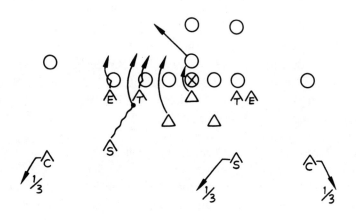

DIAGRAM 12–5.   54 Safety "7" vs. Pro

On the sprint-out pass with the right offensive end releasing, the defensive rushers have outnumbered the offensive blockers on the sprint-out pass. Both the defensive left end and tackle make contact with their keys opening up the gap for our safety blitz. Once the safety man breaks through, he is taught to get to the ball carrier as quickly as possible. The blitz man can upset the offensive maneuver in a number of ways by (1) tackling the ball, (2) disrupting the play timing, (3) making the passer throw off balance, or (4) causing the ball carrier to detour his predetermined path.

In *Diagram 12–6* of the 44 Stack defense, the defensive end to the blitz side drives into the offensive play side end, and the left defensive tackle draws the play side tackle's block. The Safety "7" Blitz puts the stunting deep defender into excellent position to make the big play with his surprise blitz.

The Monster offset stack sets up the Safety "7" Blitz perfectly,

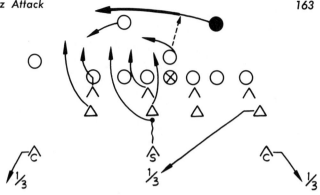

DIAGRAM 12–6. 44 Stack Safety vs. Flanker

as the left tackle shoots the gap on all fours drawing the play side tackle's cut off block. The left defensive end also steps into the right offensive end's outside shoulder opening up the "7" area. The entire Monster secondary plays man-to-man pass defense whenever the safety blitz is used. The Monster keys the right offensive end, while the backside safety man plays the left offensive end and the corner man keys the wingback man-to-man. The remaining halfback is taken by the left stacked linebacker.

The left blitzing safety positions himself slightly closer to the line of scrimmage but does not sneak up behind one of his defenders prior to the snap of the ball. The safety blitz from the Monster offset stack is more of an all out rush, with the success of the blitz depending upon the timing and speed generated by the blitzing safety man's path to the ball. The fast, direct route to the ball by the blitzer is necessitated by the secondary's man-to-man defensive pass coverage (*Diagram 12-7*).

With a veteran pass defender who possesses a great deal of football sense and has the diagnostic ability to get to the ball quickly, we

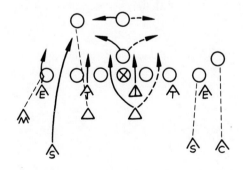

DIAGRAM 12–7. Monster Offset Stack to Man-to-Man

use a variation of the Free Safety. The Free Safety in our blitzing
secondary strategy has the freedom to blitz the opponent or to double
cover a specific pass receiving threat. Therefore, there is no preplanned path of attack for this predetermined safety man. The free
blitzing defender often upsets the offensive strategy because there is
often no rhyme or reason for his attacking a certain area. The Free
Safety's key is usually the quarterback, and his alignment and depth
is determined by the given play's defensive strategy. Regardless of the
Free Safety's alignment, the remaining defensive secondary defenders
are assigned to play a three deep nonrevolving secondary.

Diagram 12–8 points out the possible alignments and potential

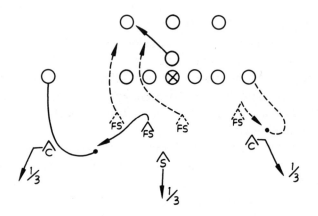

DIAGRAM 12–8.   Free Safety's Plan of Attack

routes of attack the Free Safety may wish to take, keying the sprinting-
out quarterback.

These are only a few of the many safety blitzes that may be easily
incorporated into any defensive program. By redirecting only one defender's assignment, the total defensive picture takes on a new look.

Rushing the Passer

13

One of the most spectacular plays a defender can make is tackling the passer for a big loss. In perfecting our secondary pass defense, a great deal of emphasis is placed on a well-coached pass rush program.

The best pass defense is a good rush which will either prevent the ball from being thrown or result in throwing the passer for a loss. A well-coached pass rusher is taught to tackle the passer from the top down. This means we want to tackle the passer high to interfere with his throwing an accurate pass. A passer cannot throw consistent passes lying flat on his back. If the rusher is unable to get to the passer in time to tackle him, we want our pass rushers to raise their arms high, forcing the passer to throw over the defender's raised arms or through the "picket fence." These arms may block the pass or interfere with the quarterback's vision. The defender should never jump up off his feet to block the pass because the quarterback may scramble by the rusher while the defender is in mid-air.

A strong pass rush can eliminate the long bomb and may force the passer to throw his short passes off balance. One crashing tackle by a defensive rusher may force the quarterback to get rid of the ball too quickly prior to the full development of the total pass pattern. Continual punishment by the pass rush may weaken the passer's intestinal fortitude and make him listen for the defender's footsteps.

Rushing Techniques

Speed, quickness, and agility are most important characteristics for rushing the passer. Our linebackers and ends have been our most successful rushers because these two defensive positions are selected according to the maneuverability of the defenders. Both our ends and linebackers spend a great deal of time on quickness and agility drills and can be easily taught the feinting and faking moves that a top notch defender must use in his defensive rushes.

The offensive backs have more difficulty blocking linebackers and ends because they are not rushing on passes consistently, for they also have pass defense assignments. The offensive backs are usually smaller than the linebackers and defensive ends, and both of these defenders have more distance to increase their speed and force with which to meet the offensive blocking backs.

The defensive linebackers and ends can usually out-finesse the offensive linemen who are assigned to block these rushers since the offensive blockers are often handicapped because they are bigger, less mobile, and more awkward. Our defensive coaches teach our defenders to feint and fake with either their head or shoulders on the move and to use their hands and arms to ward off the blockers. The defenders must learn to rush through the blocker's head instead of continually stepping around to the blocker's outside. All of our rushers are taught to rush from both the inside and outside angles. Usually our ends are taught to rush from the outside-in angle, but we do have some defensive calls which assign the end to rush to the inside. All of our defensive rushers are cautioned never to leave their feet in trying to block the quarterback's pass because he may decide to scramble out of his protection. Therefore, the pass rusher must come under control against a recognized scrambler.

Occasionally we want the rusher to use his power rush right over the blocker. The power rush helps to "hold" the blocker in a set position. This power rushing technique will force the blocker to set himself low in a hard-nosed position with his weight extended forward to meet power with power. This hard-nosed, off balance anticipated blocking position helps to set up the blocker for the tricky step around and inside side steps of the defender. Another highly successful method of "holding" the blocker in one set position is to use a head shoulder fake (on the run) to both the inside and then the outside; and now, the blocker is set up for the defender's finesse techniques.

We use a number of defensive rushes, and all of them may be set up by some form of a feint or a fake. But often the best fake is no fake. Faking out the pass protector may consist of faking with the rusher's legs, hips, head, or shoulders, and all of these should be perfected on the run. A good pass rusher must give the blocker time to "take the fake" before making his break toward the passer. The primary objective of the rush is a fast direct course at the target.

The rusher has the advantage over the blocker because the rules allow the defender to use his hands. On definite pass plays, we have literally pulled offensive blockers out of position in order to open up a gap for one of our other rushing defenders, à la rushing the kicker. When we pull a blocker, we use our hands to grab the opposition's jersey, pads, or arm. The defender is taught to use his hands employing a forearm blow, arm lift, stiff arm, etc.

The worst play the offense can spring on the rusher is a delayed draw or a trap play. Therefore, we give our rushers definite keys to look for to recognize these two offensive plays.

Outside Rush—The outside rush is used primarily by our ends as they are usually taught to rush the passer from an outside-in route. We want the pass rusher to combine an inside fake with his outside rush. A quick fake of the hips or shoulders to the inside or an inside step with the inside foot may help the defender elude the pass protector. Our defenders are also coached to fire directly into the blocker's outside shoulder and then to spin off to the outside to help set up future fakes. The outside rush helps to contain the passer and reduces the swing or flare passer's completion percentage.

Inside Rush—Other than depending upon an outside fake to set up the inside rush, we have found that shooting the inside gap can be the defender's best inside weapon. Whenever an offensive lineman takes a maximum split, we encourage our defender to play him slightly to his outside and then to jump back into the gap just prior to the snap of the ball and shoot the gap. Our ends and linebackers use this technique when the offensive end moves out to his split position. All of our other defensive rushers have the option of shooting the inside gap when they are certain they can beat the blocker on a definite passing down. Once the rusher has cleared the line of scrimmage, he is coached to use his outside fakes and feints to set up a direct inside route to the passer. All rushers are taught to drive straight at the blocker and whirl off to the inside to keep the blocker guessing.

Hard-Nosed Rush—The hard-nosed rush is nothing more than a power rush directly over the blocker. The head-on power rush helps to hold the blocker for future fakes. There is only one way to achieve success on the hard-nosed power rush and that is to hit the blocker with your all-out power. The defender must hit the blocker with his helmet, shoulders, forearms, legs, and hands. Keep fighting through the blocker, and if you cannot overpower him, try to go to one side or the other.

A top notch rusher must be made to realize the blocker's strategy and method of blocking on all sprint-out and pocket passes. He must know that a backfield blocker will try to maintain an inside-out angle on the defender and take him to the outside behind the passer on all straight drop-back passes. Once the defender is taught offensive pass blocking techniques and strategy, he will become a smarter and more effective pass rusher.

A top notch pass rusher must have quick feet and must be taught how to use his hands, elbows, forearms, and shoulders intelligently to tackle or ruin the rhythm of the passer. While a successful pass rush does not always tackle the passer, it may force the passer to throw off balance or to rush his pass, resulting in an interception. A good pass rusher must have finesse, quickness, football intelligence, power, and reckless viciousness to get through the maze of pass blockers. Along with a hard rush, we feel we must also combine the holding up of the potential receivers, plus pressuring all of the receivers once they have released from the line of scrimmage.

There is no perfect pass defense against a passer who is given an unlimited amount of time to throw. Therefore, we feel that our defense must place constant rushing pressure on our opposition's passing attack.

The Secondary vs.
the Running Game

14

       While we teach our deep backs to think "pass" first, we want our secondary defenders to come up quickly and make the tackle whenever a running play develops. It has been our experience in coaching that we often assume our deep defenders know the correct defensive pursuit angles to contain a sweep or attack an offensive off tackle play. Since we want to plan and practice all important phases of our defensive game, we work on our defensive pursuit angles in every one of our practice sessions.

    In discussing pursuit angles, we are not only referring to cutting off the ball carrier once he has broken away for an apparent long gainer, but also the proper attacking angles the deep backs should use in approaching the line of scrimmage. Our deep secondary backs are taught how to revolve and maintain their relative distance from their fellow defensive backs. The proper techniques and fundamentals of containing the sweep must be stressed in the field demonstrations and defensive sweeping drills.

    The defensive backs must key their assignment, take a picture of the play, and then take the proper angle on the ball carrier. The deep back must sprint up to the line of scrimmage under control and get set in a good football position so he can move in any direction. We coach our deep backs to attack the blocker aggressively using their hands and forearms to keep the blockers away from the defenders' feet. Once the defender gets rid of the blocker, he must regain his balance and be in a good football position to tackle the ball carrier.

THREE DEEP SUPPORT VS. THE RUNNING GAME

Against the interior offensive running attack, we plan to contain the opposition using an outside-in position. This means on all plays between the offensive tackles our middle safety's assignment is to meet the ball carrier head on. The two outside safety men converge on the ball carrier from their outside-in angle (*Diagram 14-1*).

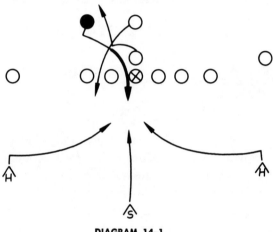

DIAGRAM 14-1.

On all running plays off the offensive tackle, our outside safety man nearest the point of attack approaches the ball carrier from the outside-in angle. The middle safety man must adjust his pursuit angle to meet the runner from an inside-out angle as close to the line of scrimmage as possible. The backside safety man must check for any possible reverse or counter action and then take a deep pursuit angle to cut off the runner if he should break loose on a long run. The backside safety must pursue cautiously looking for the ball carrier to cut back against the defensive grain. We also want this secondary defender looking for any downfield fumbles which may occur from pursuing gang tackles (*Diagram 14-2*).

Against the sweep, we want our outside safety men containing the wide play with the middle safety coming up supporting from an inside-out position. The containment against a wide or pro-type offensive formation is easier versus the sweep because our defensive perimeter and secondary defenders have established their wide alignments.

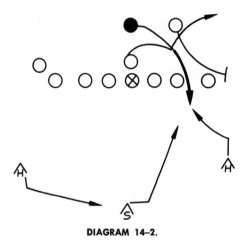

DIAGRAM 14–2.

The containing halfback must be drilled not to penetrate too deeply into the offensive backfield because he may be kicked outside opening up the funnel for the ball carrier to make his inside-outside break through the funnel (*Diagram 14-3*). The outside three deep

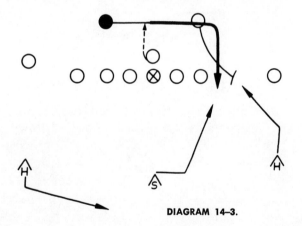

DIAGRAM 14–3.

defender must be coached to maintain the correct approach to the ball carrier and the proper position with the defensive end. The proper approach by the outside safety defender should place him on or about a yard deep into the opposition's backfield. This position will limit the blocker's chance of either kicking the safety man outside or hooking him to the inside. This correct defensive depth and approach will eliminate the opening up of the funnel for the ball carrier (*Diagram 14-4*).

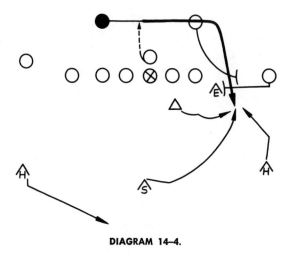

DIAGRAM 14-4.

If the ball carrier breaks outside the defensive perimeter, all of the defenders must use their inside-out pursuit angles to head off the long run (*Diagram 14-5*).

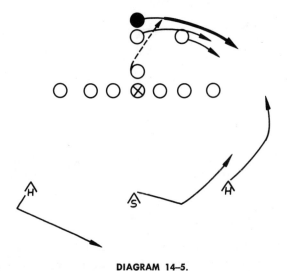

DIAGRAM 14-5.

One coaching point that must be emphasized is that the defensive end should not try to "chase" the ball carrier once he has turned the corner because the end will never catch the runner. The defensive end must retrace his steps in order to cut off the ball carrier. The middle safety man must run parallel to the ball carrier and then must be taught to set the proper pursuit angle to head off the long run.

All too often defensive coaches take players' pursuit and proper cut off angles for granted. Our coaching staff believes that this phase of secondary defense must be taught in the classroom and on the field in our defensive secondary practice sessions.

FOUR DEEP VS. THE RUNNING GAME

The four deep secondary may be used with several variations of a seven man front. The main concern of a corner or four deep secondary must be to contain the sweep. Containment of the wide running attack may be assigned to a: (1) cornerback, (2) safety man, (3) end, or (4) linebacker in a walk-away position. All of the four deep secondary alignments are concerned with fast revolvement of the deep backs with the exception of our man-to-man pass defense. Successful revolving of the deep backs must stress speed and the proper pursuit courses by the deep four defenders.

1. Containing with the Corner Man

The playside cornerback must take his proper alignment and key the frontside back through the offensive end. These two keys will signal the corner man's correct defensive path to the ball. The corner man begins to contain the sweep as soon as the frontside offensive end blocks and must never let a blocker hook him or let the ball carrier sweep around his containing position. As soon as our cornerback reaches his containing position, he is taught to squeeze the ball carrier to the inside. We call this his force-contain assignment, which prevents the ball carrier from cutting to the inside of the cornerback enabling the runner to break into the open funnel between the cornerback and the defensive end. The corner man is coached to keep his shoulders squared away to the line of scrimmage so that his outside foot will be away from the blocker.

Using the correct force-contain course, the defender actually attacks the blocker using his arms and hands to ward off the blocker (*Diagram 14-6*). We teach our cornerback to use his arms and hands on the blocker rather than his forearm because the blocker will usually use a long body rolling type of block. The forearm blow will place the defender too close to the blocker exposing his legs to a rolling type block.

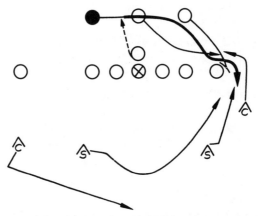

DIAGRAM 14–6.   Cornerback's Contain

The playside or onside safety man attacks the sweep physically to the inside but mentally to the outside. This means that the safety man must be ready to move quickly to the outside if the ball carrier breaks outside of our corner man's force-containing position. The safety man keys the offensive end to his side and sprints toward the line of scrimmage, locating the ball, and adjusts his pursuit course to the ball carrier's path. The safety man must continue to maintain leverage on the ball carrier and set his course to meet the ball carrier as quickly as possible (*Diagram 14-6*).

The backside or offside cornerback should revolve by gaining depth and width as soon as possible. As the sweep goes away from him, he must be thinking about the reverse or counter running plays as well as the throw-back pass. His angle of pursuit should take him on the deepest cut off course of any defender. The cornerback's pursuit angle should keep every player to his inside while he is revolving and sprinting to his pursuit channel. He must pursue under control and be looking for the ball carrier to cut back against the grain.

The backside or offside safety man must key the offensive end to his side and take a quick backward step to his outside on the snap of the ball. He must gain width and depth to cut off the ball carrier if the runner breaks through our corner defense. The backside safety man must be careful on his pursuit course so that he will not overrun the ball carrier's cut back technique.

When our corner defense attacks the option play, our defensive techniques are basically the same with our frontside corner man responsible for the pitchman (offensive running back) and the frontside (playside) safety ready to come up quickly if the quarterback keeps the ball and breaks free past the line of scrimmage.

The frontside force-contain corner man is responsible for forcing the ball carrier always to run to the inside. We tell our containing cornerback that if he forces the runner to the inside we have ten defenders ready to help tackle the ball carrier. If the ball carrier can break outside of our containment, then the runner has an open field because there are no more defenders outside to contain the ball carrier. The force-contain cornerback can never go for an inside fake because his primary defensive assignment is to contain all outside plays.

2. Containing with the Safety Man

We contain with a safety man in a Change call (invert) or to the split end's side (*Diagram 14-7*).

The reason we use a safety man contain is that we are able to attack the sweep from an inside-out angle which is a necessary change of pace along with our corner man's force-contain angle of attack. Another reason we use a safety contain is that whenever the offense sweeps to a split end our cornerback is often run off by the split end's threat on a deep pattern. Therefore, it is necessary to use our safety

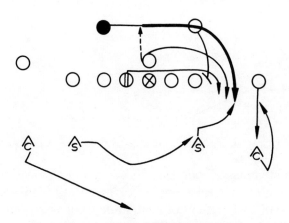

DIAGRAM 14-7. Safety Man's Contain

as the first containment and our late arriving playside corner man as a secondary contain man.

Diagram 14-7 illustrates our playside safety's containing invert angle toward the split end's side with our right corner man as a late secondary container. The left safety man's angle of pursuit is the same as described and diagrammed in containing with the cornerback. The difference is that the backside safety is depended upon to use a strong inside rush more, using the Change Call rather than the corner contain method because the invert attacking angle may place two defenders to the outside of the sweep, while the corner contain usually ends up with only the corner man as the sole container. This allows the frontside safety a better straight ahead attacking angle as compared to the frontside safety's containing assignment in a Change call.

Therefore, the Change call gives our defense another method to attack the flat area versus a sprint-out pass and a second way to attack the opposition's sweeps.

At times we use a corner secondary "look" and contain with our safety man using our cornerback as a forcing agent, whose responsibility is to make the sweeping ball carrier string out his wide maneuver. The corner man's assignment is to also force the ball carrier deeper as well as wider (*Diagram 14–8*).

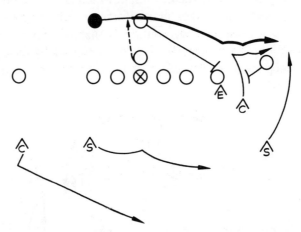

DIAGRAM 14–8. **Safety Man Contains as Cornerback Forces Ball Carrier Wider and Deeper**

The safety man still contains the sweep but now has more inside-outside forcing pursuit from our attacking corner man and defensive end. The use of this method of contain depends upon our game plan and the opposition's personnel.

3. Containing with the Defensive End

Usually when our defensive end is designated as the contain man, we are in an eight man defensive front with a three deep secondary,

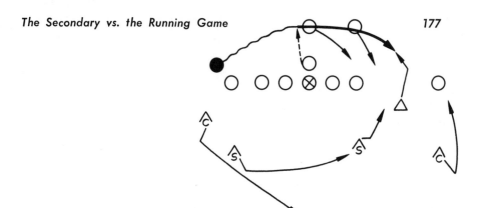

DIAGRAM 14–9.   Linebacker Contains the Sweep

which we have described earlier in this chapter. There are also special times when we assign our defensive ends the roll of container when we are using our corner or four man across the board defensive secondary.

4. Containing with the Linebacker

At times we contain with our linebacker when he is in his walk-away position. We often use our linebacker as the contain man to the split end's side whenever we use our man-to-man secondary pass call (*Diagram 14-9*).

The linebacker may also be called to contain whenever we employ our Change call and our safety is having a difficult time containing the quick sweep to his side. This would assign our linebacker as the defensive container and our safety as a secondary contain man (*Diagram 14-10*).

DIAGRAM 14–10.   Linebacker Contains the Sweep and Safety Secondary Contain

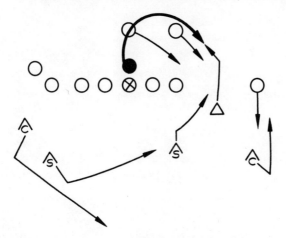

Selecting the
Secondary Defensive
Quarterback

15

Selecting the correct defensive secondary quarterback is the most important placement of personnel for the coaching staff. While many coaches may be more concerned with choosing the offensive quarterback or linebacking captain, we are more concerned with our secondary quarterback because he must make his own split second calls without the aid of the coaching staff. It is common practice today for the coaching staff to send in a large percentage of offensive plays and to flash all of the defensive interior calls from the bench. But our defensive quarterback in our secondary must recognize the formation and any motion between the few seconds when the offensive team lines up and snaps the ball. Other secondary defensive pass coverage calls may be changed depending upon offensive flow *after* the ball has been put into play. Therefore, the defensive secondary quarterback's calls are split second decisions, depending upon the formation or flow, and they cannot be signaled or carried in from the bench. The predetermined secondary calls are only used in the event that the offensive quarterback drops straight back into his pocket. Thus, the predetermined call is for the secondary's direction if a drop-back or pocket pass should occur.

The defensive secondary quarterback should know the strong points of the opposition's passing attack as well as the strong and weak points of each of our pass coverage calls. He must be a strategist and be able to anticipate the opponent's attack and their favorite sequence of passes. We want our playing secondary coordinator to constantly mix up our defensive coverage patterns as a defensive change-up in attacking the opposition's offensive planning. Our defensive secondary captain not only has the authority to attack the opponent's pass plays with an assortment of defensive calls, but he also has the power to strike against the opposition's sweeping maneuvers using a combination of unique secondary moves.

Our coaching staff believes that our defender can increase his teammates' confidence in his abilities by hard-nosed tackling and timely pass defense rather than talking. We tell our leaders that we want them to lead by action more than words.

A Signal Caller Must Be a Thinking Man

A defensive coordinator should encourage critical and creative thinking as an essential part of the defensive signal caller's learning process. Our coaching approach to calling defensive secondary signals emphasizes critical thinking, analysis, imagination, and sound judgment. The defensive quarterback should be equipped with an inquiring mind, always striving to improve his mental and physical defensive qualifications.

Selecting Defensive Quarterback's Secondary Calls

The defensive secondary quarterback's calls are based upon practice drills, scouting reports, chalk talks, ready sheets, and game films. But for split second recognition, constant practice organization must be based upon formation and passing repetition. The defensive call must be second nature to our defensive quarterback. He should have a loud, clear, and commanding voice which must be heard above the crowd noise, offensive quarterback's cadence, as well as our defensive linebacker's interior calls. All of his calls should be made with poise, which will inspire confidence in his fellow defenders.

Since the coaching staff cannot call or flash secondary signals quickly enough (based upon instant formation shifts, motion, etc.), our defensive quarterback must learn to act and think under pressure. The defensive quarterback must be coached to recognize the opposition's play sequences so that he is ready to remind his teammates of the next potential offensive maneuver. The defensive quarterback must continually study the opponent's offensive football philosophy. He should know the strong as well as the weak points of the opposition's attack. The weather, score, and field conditions should influence the quarterback's defensive pass coverage calls.

We want our defensive signal caller to recognize and react to all types of motion, split ends, flankers, slot backs, etc. Therefore, the head coach and the defensive backfield coach must continually check and quiz the secondary quarterback pertaining to his defensive coverage calls. We demand that our defensive quarterback study offensive football as well as our own defensive football program.

The defensive secondary captain must constantly review the strategic situations concerning the score and the amount of time left in the game. He must memorize how many time-outs we have left, as well as how many time-outs our opponents have left in the game. Field condition, down, and hash mark positions are of utmost importance to make the proper defensive calls.

Defensive Quarterback's Qualifications

Since the passing game has increased in popularity, in high schools and colleges, a greater stress must be placed on the defensive secondary. To lead or quarterback the defensive secondary, the choice should be a young man who has a winning attitude. He must be willing to work on his basic defensive secondary calls, as well as his physical defensive pass techniques throughout the year. This defender must have pride, confidence, and be a sixty minute competitor.

The most desirable physical qualifications of course would be size, quickness, and agility. But we will take an average sized football player who has lateral quickness plus the burning desire to prepare to be the best defensive leader. He must be intelligent with the ability to make quick confident decisions.

Communicating

A highly successful pass defense is a talking defense. Our defensive secondary signal caller must be able to communicate among his fellow players in the huddle and during the actual game action. In the huddle he makes his predetermined calls concerning the direction of our rotation if a balanced formation may show and the offensive quarterback uses a straight drop-back pass. We coach our defensive quarterback to stress the "big play" by emphasizing the down and distance situations. A warning, "Bob, watch the sideline and go pattern," may be the personal key that will help one of our defenders make a key defensive play.

During all time-outs, we request our defensive secondary captain to come over to the sidelines to discuss any new strategic situations that may have arisen in the last few minutes. Continual communications between the coach and the defensive quarterback will help to answer many of his future decisions and will give him the necessary confidence so he may continue to make his sound judgment calls.

The third down and must maneuver by our opposition's offense is the most important defensive play we must make. All of our defensive coaches review their most consistent third down plays and discuss the offensive third down attack with our defensive secondary leader. As a staff, we feel that our defensive strategy must cover and anticipate any possible problem that may confront our defensive secondary signal caller. Next we must review any anticipated situation which may develop, so that our secondary captain can make the best possible call. If he is ever in doubt as to the correct call, we tell him to call time out and to confer with our coaches during the time-out period.

The defensive secondary quarterback is taught to use the percentage secondary call against the anticipated offensive maneuvers. Therefore, we want to attack our opponent with our most consistent defensive performer on all "big play" or clutch situations.

The number of teaching-learning situations are countless for our defensive quarterback to analyze. But we concentrate on the key third and long and third and short situations along with our goal line secondary calls. These clutch situations are covered and reviewed each day during our preseason drills, so that our defensive signal caller is ready to handle our overall defensive secondary game plan prior to our first encounter.

Our defensive quarterback is continually quizzed concerning the game's rules. It is our defensive signal caller's job to make all of our penalty calls. The defensive quarterback must also recognize the value of the clock on our overall defensive game planning. Our defensive quarterback's manual covers all of the various methods on the "hows" and "whys" of using the clock to our secondary's advantage.

The coaching staff designates the defensive quarterback to call time out for our defense. We review the ten important reasons for calling defensive time-outs before our first game. These problems are:

1. New offensive alignment
2. Injury
3. Equipment change
4. Conserve time
5. Defensive Quarterback—Coach strategy sideline meeting
6. Personnel change
7. Check assignments
8. Morale problem
9. Team rest period
10. Opponent's offensive breaking away for consistent gainers.

The defensive quarterback must be well rounded in the type of defensive secondary we are using. There are two types of secondaries: One is an attacking secondary and the other is a containing defense.

He should know the opposition's basic pass patterns from all of the offensive formations and be ready to make the correct secondary call immediately. In calling our secondary change-up stunts, the defensive signal caller should know the offensive tendencies from each formation. Therefore, we want our defensive secondary quarterback to anticipate a particular pass or running play and make his "stunting" secondary call. Intelligent anticipation and sound execution are the keynotes of a successful secondary defense.

Most of our stunting defensive secondary calls are made after the ball has been put into play because the offense's movement from a particular alignment often dictates the area the opposition plans to strike. All of the opposition's maneuvers from each formation have been totaled for frequency and percentages in our scouting reports and game plan. Therefore, we can teach our defensive quarterback to anticipate a specific tendency from the totaled tendencies that have shown up on our coach's scouting report.

We help to disguise our stunts from our secondary by lining up in our four man across the board and move one or two of our deep backs just prior to the snap of the ball. The only way we can achieve success in attacking our opponent's offense is through repetition in practice and under game-like conditions. If the scout team will run the anticipated offense plays just as our next opponents run them, our defensive secondary will be able to react and attack these same plays successfully during the game.

During our practice sessions, we have found that a valuable coaching point in teaching our defensive quarterback the overall opponent's sweeping and passing philosophy is to actually have our defensive signal caller play the offensive quarterback and the primary receiver. In emulating these opponents, our defensive quarterback learns the opponent's offensive attack by "doing" rather than through play recognition, blackboard chalk talks, or viewing the opposition's films.

The final defensive game plan must be completed by Wednesday. Our staff uses Monday and Tuesday for experimenting with our anticipated game plan. Thursday and Friday are used by our defense as review days, and Friday evening the defensive quarterback is given the opportunity to explain our defensive secondary game plan to our entire defense and defensive coaching staff. We give our defensive quarterback the assignment of explaining our defensive secondary strategy because our staff believes that any defender who can teach our attacking strategy can successfully make our correct defensive calls.

Once the coaching staff has selected its two or three basic secondary calls for the next opponent, there are several offensive ideas we must consider in our game plan against the opposition's passing attack. We have listed some basic offensive information that should be pertinent to our defensive quarterback's game strategy.

1. What type of pass patterns are used by our opponent?
   a. Drop-back passes
   b. Play-action passes
   c. Sprint-out passes
   d. Pull-up passes
2. What is the favorite style of opposition's pass offense flood passes, divide passes, isolation patterns?
3. How much time does their passer need to throw?
4. Who is their poorest pass blocker?
5. What type of pass blocking do they use?
6. Who is their best passer?
7. Who is their favorite receiver?
8. What is their favorite third down "must" pass?
9. Who is their fastest wide receiver?
10. Who is their favorite backfield receiver?
11. Which receiver is primarily a blocker?

12. What is their favorite long bomb pattern?
13. What is their favorite short yardage pass?
14. What is their favorite screen pass?
15. What is their favorite draw play?
16. What is their favorite pass-run option play?

Selecting Man-to-Man Secondary Personnel

Outside Corner Men—These two defenders should be two of the fastest and quickest members of the secondary. They must be able to cover the opponent's top receiver man to man because the opposition will try to isolate their top threat on our outside defender. Our corner defenders are responsible for more area than our inside pass defender.

Inside Safety Men—The safety men must be two of our top defensive tacklers. We select our safety men primarily for their quickness rather than their straight away speed. One of these two deep defenders may be free to roam like a center fielder because their offensive keys (tight end or running back) are often used as blockers.

Our four deep man-to-man defense must become a smooth working team unit. Each defender should know each other's assignments on all calls so that our entire unit understands the full meaning and strategy behind each defensive pass call. The defensive quarterback must completely digest each scouting report and know the strong and weak points of all his fellow pass defenders.

All four deep defenders should talk to each other pertaining to the opposition's attacking strategy. If one of the corner men is in an in-between position between the tight end and flanker, the safety man over the flanker must warn him whenever the flanker begins to crack back on the cornerback. All man-to-man pass defenders must talk up crossing ends, pick off passes, draws, and screen plays. A solid confident pass defense is a talking defense.

Selecting Invert Secondary Personnel

Outside Deep Pass Defenders—The two wide outside defenders must have speed and agility to defend against the isolated one on one pass patterns by the flankers or the split ends. The wide corner defenders must have the quickness to cover the outside flag and sideline cuts. If the wide receivers make inside short cuts, the linebacker may help out the wide defensive back, while the free inside safety man is assigned to help out on the deep inside cuts. One pass cut that must be repeatedly practiced between the outside corner defender and the inside safety is the deep post cut. Since on all zone calls the outside defenders are assigned their outside one-third zone, they must have the speed to cover the deepest receiver's many deep patterns.

Inside Deep Pass Defenders—The inside safety defenders must be hard-nosed tacklers and have the ability to diagnose the offensive backfield maneuvers. One maneuver the two inside safeties must be able to recognize is the bootleg play. If one of the safety men misplay this action, it will leave the deep middle defensive zone open for the long home run pass. The inside safety men must have both the physical and the mental quickness to cover either the flat or the deep middle zone, depending upon either the secondary call, action of the quarterback, or their key recognition.

Pass Defense Practice

16

In our practice sessions we emphasize the same fundamental techniques which we use in grading our game films. We stress the deep back's alignment, reaction, position on the receiver and interception path. The most important fundamental listed above is for the defensive back to always have the proper position on the intended receiver. We teach these fundamental techniques in individual, group, and team drills.

Our coaching staff believes the only method of teaching pass defense is not to yell, "You missed the interception," because the defender knows that. Rather, we point out that the reason the defender missed the ball was that his approach course was incorrect.

The staff's teaching philosophy features the whole method of learning. This philosophy gives the player the complete picture so he will understand the purpose of reasoning behind a particular coaching point.

All of our secondary defensive drills are kept brief and changed often to eliminate boredom among our defensive backs. Most of our drills are actual football drills which attempt to emulate actual game-like conditions. Our defensive secondary drills are organized to be as competitive as possible.

Each practice segment is planned and organized in advance as our practice time is limited. Our defensive secondary pass sessions are planned to develop the defensive skills necessary for a winning secondary unit. All of our practice sessions are followed by a classroom or field blackboard review period. At the end of each defensive pass call unit, each player is quizzed mentally and physically in the correct fundamental and technical secondary skills.

In this chapter we have discussed our defensive pass practice organization plan through each day of the week. This outline includes Monday's scouting report review through Friday's total review practice plan. This week's day by day practice plan is essentially the same throughout our entire week's pregame schedule.

This weekly practice plan is formulated by the defensive secondary coach, which helps to instill in an assistant coach personal pride in organizing and carrying out this weekly schedule.

PASS DEFENSE PRACTICE ORGANIZATION

Monday

Coordinate all secondary pass calls by opponent's formations and our defensive line calls. Work to improve our previous game's weak points. Our defensive pass coach discusses our basic defensive pass attack for next week.

Prior to Monday's practice, our pass defensive coach draws cards of the opponent's pass plays for the scout team to run. A demonstration team jogs through opposition's favorite calls against our basic defensive secondary calls. During this practice period we preview the opposition's favorite pass plays according to down, distance, and field position.

We give the answers to our secondary and linebackers concerning:

1. What is their big third down "Possession Play"?
2. What is their basic short yardage pass?
3. What is their basic long yardage pass?
4. Who is their favorite long receiver?
5. Who is their favorite short receiver?
6. What type of a passer do we face this week?

Monday's practice is often in sweats; therefore, we jog through our secondary call versus our opponent's formation pertaining to: Personnel, alignments, keys, and responsibilities.

Our pass defense coaching points for the day are:

1. Stress quickness and reaction in all drills.
2. Emphasize mental preparation for our next encounter.
3. Only work against opposition's favorite passes.

Tuesday

Work especially against the roll-out and sprint-out pass actions. Check our outside blitz stunts against these actions. Coordinate our pass rush and coverage especially toward the split end side. Make sure our defenders are attacking the running plays using their correct angles.

Review our defensive pass calls against their favorite pass patterns. Make certain the scout team is running the opponent's pass patterns correctly. Tuesday is the day we add any new assignment or call into our overall defensive plans. During this period the coach may direct the passer to throw the pass directly at the defender to give the defenders a more positive approach to their respective assignments.

Tuesday's pass defense coaching points include incorporating the defender's footwork and reaction for each secondary call. We also review all our pass coverage calls we plan to use for next week's opponent. The pass defense coach emphasizes each defender to go through the receiver's head while making a bona fide attempt to intercept the pass.

This is the day we pass out the Secondary Ready Sheets for our defenders. On Tuesday noon the defensive coaches have lunch with our defensive quarterbacks. During lunch we review our total defensive philosophy for the week and go over the opponent's attacking strategy.

Wednesday

Work on the entire short passing game with our linebackers and secondary. Review all anticipated play-action passes. All motion plays are run through by the demonstration team and we go over our calls to motion as well as our defensive adjustments prior to the snap of the ball.

Wednesday we go over our goal line pass defense adjustments, coordinating our pass rush with our secondary calls. A spirit, hustling, and positive approach prevails during our defensive goal line segment. All of the opponent's goal line pass plays and tendencies are reviewed during this period.

This middle of the week practice session is when we go over our linebacker's adjustments to wide formations. The opposition's passing situations are reviewed by formations. The linebackers' blitzes are co-ordinated with our secondary calls. The defensive alignments and calls are emphasized to the flanker's side. We continually question our pass defenders concerning their alignment, calls, and responsibilities. The defender's running and pass action keys are tested during a combination running and passing drill period. This is the day we work on the short passing game. We use a combination of blitzes, holding up the receivers and maximum pass defenders to change-up on the passer. These techniques are used against both the short and the long passing attack.

Our tackling fundamentals are reviewed with emphasis upon the perfect tackle drill. We also use the one-on-one technique in three yard squares as well as tackling the machine on occasion. The coaching points we stress in all our tackling drills are:

1. Approach
2. Position
3. Contact
4. Follow Through

Thursday

On Thursday our pass defense should be sharp, reaching near perfection. We expect a spirit secondary drill day as it is our last contact prior to Saturday's encounter. This is the day we concentrate on the opponent's top drop-back passes. It is imperative that our linebackers' and safety blitzes up the middle are successful against the pocket passing attack. While we do favor the middle blitzes, we also hold up the favorite receivers on sure passing downs. We feel that a weekly review on this day of our Victory or Prevent Pass Defense is a necessity. Concentration is also placed on our linebacker's hook zone and man-to-man coverage. "Draw Action Passes" are also used to keep our linebackers honest.

Work on the flood pass and short passing attack is stressed. We use preplanned intercepted passes where we overload the pass defense to underline a solid optimistic approach to our total pass defense program. We work on our inside-outside defensive coverage techniques, emphasizing the correct pursuit course against the run or a completed pass.

This is test day and our coverage and secondary calls must be sharp at the end of the day. We review our entire pass defense strategy coordinating our total pass coverage and pass rush defense.

Coaching Point: Test defenders on Ready Sheet.

Friday

Squad prepractice quiz by the head coach pertaining to opponent's favorite formations and our line and secondary calls. Friday is also the day the defensive secondary coach should answer any questions our defenders may have concerning our coverage or the opposition's formation tendencies. We run through all of our calls against all of the opposition's expected formations. We also quickly review our Victory and Spread Calls against our demonstrators.

Coaching Point: The secondary's positive approach must prevail through this abbreviated practice session. We emphasize: When the ball is in the air . . . *It's ours!* Our defense may bend, but it will never break. We shall intercept at least three of our opponent's passes.

All pass defenders should close out Friday's session with an interception to maintain their confidence.

PRACTICE TEACHING PROGRESSION

1. Explain basic zone or man-to-man pass defense
   a. Walk through assignments
   b. Answer questions of players
   c. Ask questions if players lack questions
2. Run through basic pass defense call
   a. Run individual offensive pass patterns
   b. Teach individual coaching points
   c. Answer players' questions
3. Run "Big Three" most difficult pass patterns
   a. Limit pass to throw within 3.7 seconds in group drills
   b. Emphasize footwork
   c. Concentrate on attacking the sweep
4. Work on sprint-out and pass-action passes
   a. Emphasize player's position for tackle or playing the ball
   b. Be a talking defense especially when the passer sprints out beyond the tackle's box
   c. Sprint when the ball is in the air

5. Progress to most difficult pass patterns
   a. Emphasize interceptions in team drills
   b. Go through receiver for interception
   c. Build confidence by "buying" off offense passer and receivers
6. Work on game condition drills
   a. Footwork drills
   b. Position drills
   c. Interception drills

Pass Defense
Drills

17

A well-coached pass defense is a defense that can execute successfully. Execution comes from constant practice, and we improve our pass defense by repetition through our individual, group, and team drills.

Excellent defensive secondary drills must be well conceived and meaningful to all of our pass defenders. All of our defensive pass drills simulate actual game conditions and in this way are more interesting and meaningful to our defenders.

All of our secondary drills must accomplish one of the following four phases:

1. Tackle the pass receiver.
2. Knock down the intended pass.
3. Intercept the pass.
4. Tackle the running back.

Formation Cards

All offensive formations that we expect to meet are diagrammed on fifteen by twenty inch (15″ × 20″) cards. These cards are used as recognition for our defensive quarterback to test his coverage calls.

Play Cards

All of the pass plays that we may face are illustrated on fifteen by twenty inch (15″ × 20″) cardboard cards. The opponent team runs the pass plays diagrammed on these cards against our defenses. We diagram all of our opposition's passes with motion and shifting adjustments. We save these cards for teaching our next year's varsity players in the spring. These cards are again reviewed in the early summer two-a-day practice sessions. These play cards are also used off the field in the classroom during our chalk talks.

Teaching Drills

We use a series of progressive drills that lead up to a particular secondary skill. Each individual, group, and team drill progresses through to the ultimate concept we are teaching.

Group drills are used after the defensive players have been introduced to their individual secondary drills. Group drills are stressed as soon as we begin to play our game schedule. These drills help the individual player to recognize his teammates' assignments and the importance of secondary team play.

While we use both man-to-man and zone pass defense, 75 percent of our drills are man-to-man drills because we feel it is easier to teach zone pass defense after using man-to-man principles, than to teach man-to-man coverage after first teaching zone. Actually, playing the ball and maintaining the correct cushion is relatively the same using either defensive pass coverage.

In introducing man-to-man secondary drills, we teach our individual man-to-man defensive fundamentals and techniques without using the football. This is especially true in our shadow drills.

Regardless of the fact that we may have called a zone pass defense, we still employ man-to-man pass defense principles because more and more passing attacks are attempting to isolate a receiver in a given area.

REACTION DRILLS

Physical and mental reactions can be developed through selected reaction drills. A defensive back can learn quickness through the proper defensive pass drills. The purpose of all reaction drills is to make the defender's timing sharper using a drill which resembles a given game situation. We continually search for drills which feature total reactions.

KEY FOR PASS DEFENSE DRILL DIAGRAMS

V   **Defender**

○   **Offensive Player**

●   **Passer**

⊗   **Center**

▽   **Coach**

⦸   **Dummy**

⟶   **Offensive Course**

∿⟶   **Defensive Course**

----➤   **Pass**

Our staff always likes to finish our reaction drills on an enthusiastic, positive note, making an individual or group look good by "stacking the deck" in favor of the defense.

MAN-TO-MAN OPTIONAL CUT DRILL (Diagram 17-1)

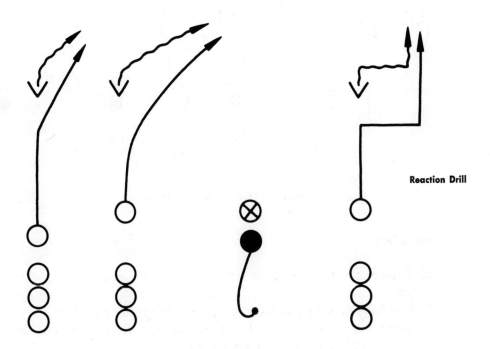

Reaction Drill

DIAGRAM 17–1.   Man-to-Man Optional Cut Drill

Execution:

1. Set up three lines of receivers (split end, flanker, and tight end) to run option cuts.
2. Pass defenders are assigned to cover pass receivers on their individual cuts.
3. Quarterback has only three seconds to throw the ball or the play is counted as an incomplete pass.
4. Pass receivers are limited to only two fakes.

Coaching Points:

A quick man-to-man drill, that combines all of the important defender's reaction, position, and footwork fundamentals, is necessary for consistently sound defensive secondary man-to-man pass defense.

INSIDE-OUTSIDE DRILL (Diagram 17-2)

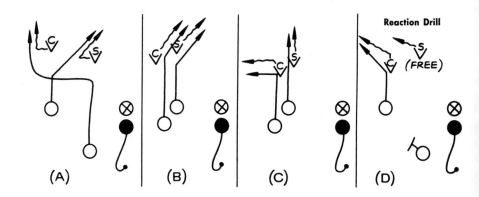

DIAGRAM 17–2.   Inside-Outside Drill

Execution:

1. Teaches the Inside-Outside defensive pass responsibilities for our players.
2. Receivers must line up tight or within a five to six yard area.
3. Safety man first makes call and outside defender must return the call to confirm the safety's suggestion.

4. If two receivers release:
   (a) Safety takes inside receiver
   (b) Corner takes outside receiver
       (Diag. 17–2A)
5. Both receivers cut to the inside:
   (a) Safety takes deepest
   (b) Corner takes shortest
       (Diag. 17–2B)
6. Both receivers break outside:
   (a) Safety takes deepest
   (b) Corner takes shortest
       (Diag. 17–2C)
7. Only one receiver releases:
   (a) Safety is free to play the ball
   (b) Corner plays the man
       (Diag. 17–2D)

Coaching Points:

This drill teaches Inside-Outside zone coverage within our Man-to-Man coverage call. It helps teach defenders to key both receivers prior to final pass pattern cuts.

IN-BETWEEN DRILL (Diagram 17-3)

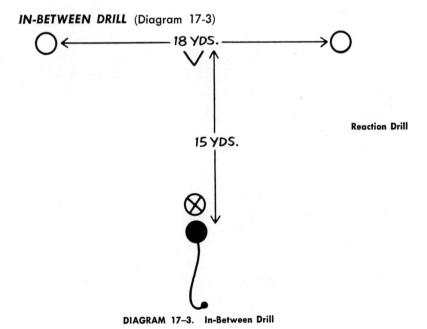

DIAGRAM 17–3.   In-Between Drill

Execution:

1. Begin with two stationary receivers eighteen yards apart and a defender between the receivers.
2. Fifteen yards away the passer should take a snap and sprint back another six yards and throw to either receiver.
3. After every three passes, the passer should move his center back five yards.
4. This increases the distance between the passer and the receivers and affords the defender more of a chance to get to the ball.

Coaching Points:

Adds confidence to the pass defender by proving to him how many more yards he can cover as we increase the distance between the passer and the receiver.

FOOTWORK DRILLS

Most of our drills place the emphasis upon covering an isolated defender, using back pedalling and shuffle steps to cover the receiver. We want our pass defender to keep most of his weight on the balls of his feet so he can move quickly in any direction. Once the pass receiver gets within two yards of the secondary receiver, the defender must forget his back pedalling and begin to turn and sprint with the receiver. The pass defender is coached to watch the receiver's arms and attack the ball once the receiver raises his arms to make the catch.

SHADOW DRILL (Diagram 17-4)

Execution:

1. Divide the field into thirds and place a pass defender and receiver into each divided area.
2. The defensive man shadows the receiver forty yards down field keeping a comfortable cushion on the receiver.
3. The coach does not use a football in this drill but only watches the defender's footwork.

4. At the end of the forty yards, the defender exchanges position and assignments with the offensive receiver.

Coaching Points:

Enables the defenders to concentrate on their footwork and cushion without the added responsibility of playing the ball. Good early season introductory drill for man-to-man coverage.

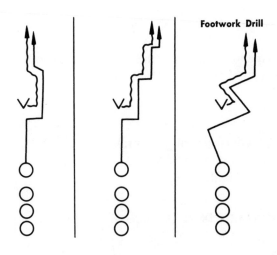

DIAGRAM 17–4. Shadow Drill

BACK PEDALLING DRILL (Diagram 17-5)

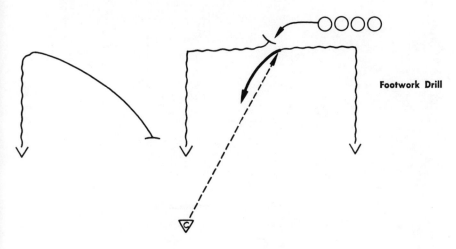

DIAGRAM 17–5. Back Pedalling Drill

Execution:

1. Defenders line up ten yards apart and six yards away from the passer.
2. All of the defenders call, "Pass," and begin to shuffle backward for fifteen yards.
3. Then the passer throws the ball into the seam between the pass defenders about fifteen yards deep.
4. When one defender calls for the ball, the other defender peels to block the intended receiver who is stationed a few yards behind the play.
5. The interceptor intercepts the ball at its highest position, puts the ball away, and then runs for daylight.

Coaching Points:

The defenders are taught to take short, choppy, controlled steps backward, maintaining a wide base with the ability to move in any direction for the ball.

MAN-ON-MAN DRILL (Diagram 17-6)

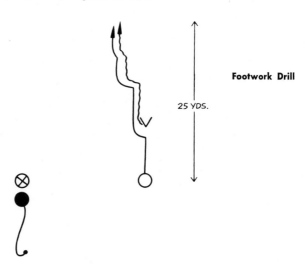

Footwork Drill

25 YDS.

DIAGRAM 17–6.   Man-on-Man Drill

Execution:

1. Pass defender is stationed six yards off the line of scrimmage.
2. Defender should shade receiver's inside or outside shoulder.
3. Pass defender must stay with the receiver for twenty-five yards.
4. Have defender maintain his proper leverage and cushion on pass receiver.
5. Pass defender should focus eyes on receiver looking for the ball only when the receiver raises his hands for the ball.
6. Maintain a position so the defender can look through the receiver to the ball.

Coaching Points:

This is what pass defense is all about—man-on-man. This drill should be used throughout the season, giving the pass receiver his option of pass patterns.

POSITION ON THE RECEIVER

Good position is the secret key to success in all sports, particularly in football's pass defense. If a pass defender does not have good position on a receiver, it is a potential six point play for the offense.

By the proper position on the receiver, the author does not mean only the defender's position staying between the intended receiver and the goal line, but the actual cushion position and the specific defender's body position on the receiver going up for the ball.

The defensive secondary coach must teach the defender to go through the receiver for the ball. He must teach our deep defenders to make solid contact with the receiver while making a bona fide attempt to intercept the ball. Therefore, we have selected three of our most successful position on the receiver drills to help demonstrate the dog fight between the defender and the receiver going after the football.

LEVELING OFF DRILL (Diagram 17-7)

Execution:

1. Defender lines up six yards deep and attacks the receiver's sideline route.

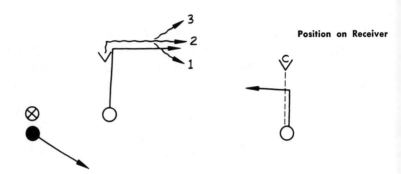

DIAGRAM 17–7.   Leveling Off Drill

2. Receiver runs straight down field for eight yards and then runs a sideline cut.
3. Defender makes his break on the "long arm" action of the sprint-out quarterback, going for the ball all the way.
4. Passer throws the ball in one of three areas:
   (a) In front of the receiver.
   (b) Slightly in front of the receiver.
   (c) Behind the receiver.
5. Gives the defender a view of the passer through the receiver and helps to teach him to take away the all-important sideline pass pattern.

Coaching Points:

Teaches defender to go through the receiver for the ball. Keeps the receivers and passer and the ball within the defender's views.

OFFENSE VS. DEFENSE SCORING DRILL (Diagram 17-8)

Execution:

1. Six offensive players run their pass offense against six defensive pass defenders.
2. Passer must throw within 3.7 seconds.
3. Defense may use zone, man-to-man, or combo call.
4. Ball should be placed on each hash mark to emulate actual game conditions.

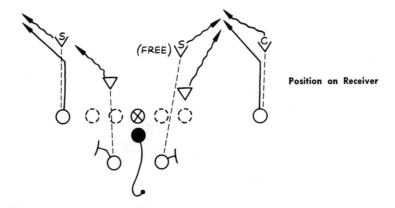

(FREE)

Position on Receiver

DIAGRAM 17–8. Offense vs. Defense Scoring Drill

5. Team Scoring:
   Offense: Two points for each completion.
   Twenty-five points for each touchdown pass.
   Defense: One point each incomplete pass or pass not thrown within 3.7 seconds.
   Two points each pass knocked down.
   Five points each pass interception.
   Twenty-five points each interception for a touchdown.

Coaching Points:

Helps to build teamwork among units through a highly competitive drill. Any time a coach keeps score, players seem to increase their reaction timing.

PLAY THE BALL DRILL (Diagram 17-9)

Execution:

1. The coach is the passer and will set up in three different drop-back courses:
   (a) Sprint-out right
   (b) Drop-back pocket action
   (c) Sprint-out left

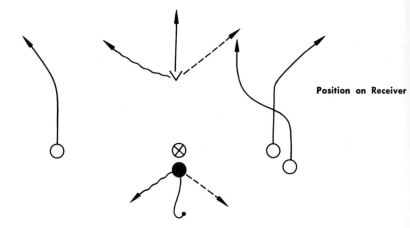

Position on Receiver

DIAGRAM 17–9.   Play the Ball Drill

2. As the passer drops back, the defender begins to cover the zone depending upon the quarterback's drop-back or sprint-out action.
3. The passer reacts to the passer's "long arm" action.
4. Passer throws the ball and defender sprints to the ball.
5. Defender must use a straight line path to make the interception because the shortest distance between two points is a straight line.

Coaching Points:

Teaches player to get to the ball, make his interception call, and catch the ball at its highest point.

TIP DRILLS

All of our pass defenders practice our tip drills. Deflected passes are increasing each year with the employment of multi-changing secondary calls, blitzing defenses, and the emphasis upon taller rushing defenders with upraised arms.

Our three selected deflected pass drills teach the defender to react to game situations which often occur from various defensive angles and positions. As many as one-fourth of our pass interceptions resulted from tipped or batted passes.

Quickness, agility, and reactions are all assets which may be developed through the proper use of selected deflection drills. Our defensive coaches agree with the Pasturean theory that, "chance favors a prepared mind;" therefore, we prepare our defenders for deflected passes which may result in a key interception through our selected tip drills.

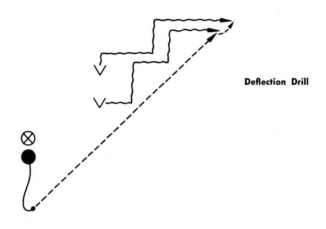

Deflection Drill

DIAGRAM 17–10. Wave—Tip Drill

Execution:

1. Quarterback drops back and fakes the ball in several different directions before passing.
2. First defender lines up four yards deep and the second defender lines up seven yards deep and both react to passer's fakes.
3. Second defender should always be behind the first defender by three or more yards.
4. Passer throws to first defender who is the tipper, and he tips the ball to the second defender.
5. Second defender intercepts the ball at its highest point, puts it away, and then runs with it.

Coaching Points:

Teaches defender to play tipped or batted ball in relatively the same position as he does during the game.

THREE LINE TIP DRILL (Diagram 17-11)

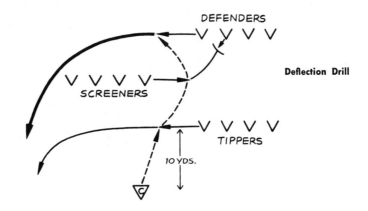

DIAGRAM 17–11.   Three Line Tip Drill

Execution:

1. Passer throws the ball to the tip man who bats the ball into the air.
2. The second line of screeners can tip, fake a tip, and throw their hands up just in front of the interceptor.
3. The interceptor must maintain a position where he can make the play regardless of the tip and the second effort of the screener.
4. The tip and the screen lines help to force the defender to concentrate on the football.
5. We change the players' parallel lines to vertical lines so that the defenders may have a chance to intercept the ball from a variety of angles.

Coaching Points:

This drill teaches the defender the proper position and body control needed to be in the correct place to make the interception.

HEAD-ON TIP DRILL (Diagram 17-12)

Execution:

1. Defenders line up in straight line.
2. Passer throws ball six yards away from tip man with partner following four yards behind tipper.

3. First man tips the ball high into the air, to the side or low.
4. Passer throws passes softly so they can all be batted into the air by tipper.
5. Second defender concentrates on the deflected football and makes the interception at its highest point. Then returns to line as the tipper.

Coaching Points:

Teaches defenders to intercept batted or deflected ball.

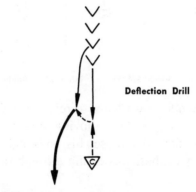

Deflection Drill

DIAGRAM 17–12.   Head-On Tip Drill

INTERCEPTION DRILLS

All of our defenders are told to yell, "Pass," once the quarterback cocks his arm to throw. The pass defender sprints to his point, widens his base, and comes under control, getting set to make the interception. The pass defender is taught to intercept the ball at its highest point. Once the defender is in the correct defensive position, we want him to intercept the ball, put it away, and then run with it.

INTERCEPTION ANGLE DRILL (Diagram 17-13)

Execution:

1. Since many coaches use only the wave interception drill, the defender always intercepts the ball moving away from the passer.
2. We use four angle phases we want our pass defenders to practice when going for an interception.

Interception Drill

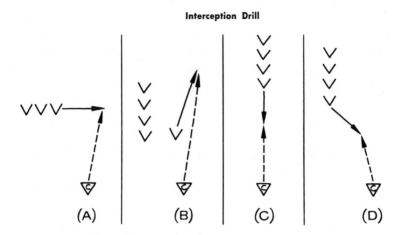

DIAGRAM 17–13.   Interception Angle Drill

3. The pass defender must learn to relax his hands and to concentrate on any pass as long as he is moving toward the ball.
4. We want the defender to get his body behind the ball if possible because many of these passes slip through the secondary defender's hands.

Coaching Points:

Pass defenders experience intercepting the ball from all of the angles they will face in game situations.

DOG FIGHT DRILL (Diagram 17-14)   **Interception Drill**

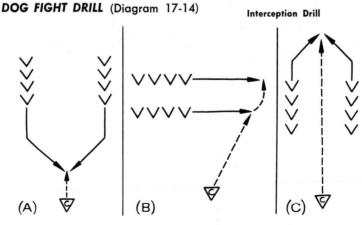

DIAGRAM 17–14.   Dog Fight Drill

Execution:

1. This drill uses the forward, parallel, and backward directions a defender must use for the interception.
2. The passer should be fifteen yards away from the spot of the intended dog fight.
3. The pass defender must be alert and ready to go for the pass at its highest point and he must learn to time his jumps.
4. Players are encouraged to keep score between themselves and encourage the competition between defenders.
5. Makes sure the defender keeps his eyes on the ball.
6. "Intercept the ball, put it away, and then run with it," are our coaching terms in this drill.

Coaching Points:

The Dog Fight Drills teach the defenders to battle each other for the ball using their hips, arms, shoulders, hands, and head. The three directions help to acquaint the players with the various flights and direction of the ball and emphasizes the second effort aspect of pass defense.

CIRCLE DRILL (Diagram 17-15)

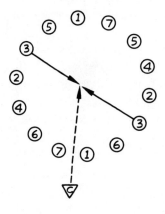

Interception Drill

DIAGRAM 17–15. Circle Drill

Execution:

1. Players line up in a circle.
2. Coach assigns each player a number and calls out two or possibly three numbers and throws the ball into the center of the circle.
3. The players whose numbers are called sprint to the ball and fight each other for the interception.
4. All of the players may hold hands or air dummies, and those players whose numbers are not called will hit the interceptor with a jolt.
5. This jolt habitizes the intercepting defender to a sudden hit following his interception.

Coaching Points:

Helps to develop competition and pride among the pass defenders by going up and fighting for the interception. Teaches the defender to use his hips, shoulders, and elbows while making a bona fide attempt for the ball.

TACKLING

The game of football is a contact sport consisting of blocking and tackling; therefore, on defense we emphasize hard-nosed tackling by our secondary defender.

All good defensive football players must be well schooled in the fundamentals of solid tackling. We teach our defenders four basic phases of tackling:

1. Approach—The defender must come under control just prior to making contact. This means he must gather himself, with his feet up under himself, and his eyes fixed on the ball carrier.

2. Position—The tackler must maintain a good football position with his weight on the balls of his feet and ready to uncoil from his hitting football position.

3. Contact—We teach our tackler to glue his eyes on the target and drive through this point. He should drive his forehead into the ball carrier, uncoiling all his force from his power producing angles of his feet and legs. He should wrap his arms around the ball carrier and keep his feet driving through the target.

4. Follow Through—The tackler must keep driving his legs until the ball carrier is grounded. The defender must continue to keep his arms around the ball carrier until both hit the ground or the whistle blows.

OPEN FIELD SHED—TACKLE DRILL (Diagram 17-16)

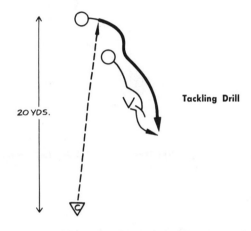

DIAGRAM 17–16. Open Field Shed—Tackle Drill

Execution:

1. Coach passes ball twenty yards down field to receiver who is assigned a blocker to escort him up field.
2. Defender is stationed ten yards away and is coached to shed the blocker and take the correct angle to make the tackle.
3. Defender is taught to run the ball carrier into the sidelines by taking an advantageous angle approach.
4. The defender must use his arms and use a head and shoulder fake to get rid of the lead blocker.
5. The defensive man is coached to butt the ball carrier rather than tackle him because we are teaching the proper position, footwork, and hitting techniques.

Coaching Points:

One of the most overlooked aspects of secondary play is attacking the open field ball carrier with a blocker in front of him. This gives the defender the needed confidence of stopping the open field runner.

SIDELINE TACKLING DRILL (Diagram 17-17)

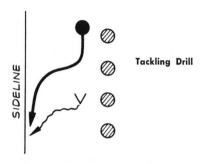

DIAGRAM 17–17.   Sideline Tackling Drill

Execution:

1. Ball carrier makes a break for the sidelines and the defender is taught to take the proper pursuit angle.
2. The defender is instructed to use the sidelines to his advantage by running and tackling the ball carrier out of bounds.
3. Give the ball carrier only one alternative of running straight between the sidelines and ball carrier.
4. Don't leave your feet on the tackle but tackle through the ball carrier, driving him out of bounds.
5. Keep your head in front of the ball carrier.

Coaching Points:

This drill can be used at full or three-quarter speed and gives defender confidence in his tackling ability.

SKELETON TACKLING DRILL (Diagram 17-18)

Execution:

1. Defensive secondary lines up in their multi-alignment sets and attacks the offensive sweeps.

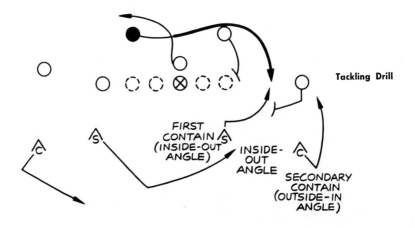

DIAGRAM 17–18. Skeleton Tackling Drill

2. The offense runs sweep to both sides and the defensive secondary attacks with the correct angles from their particular defensive alignments.

3. Occasionally we tell our defensive receivers to release down field and run a quarterback sweep. This makes the defensive secondary defenders drop back first for the possible pass and then react to the sweeping ball carrier.

4. Later we add our defensive ends to teach our defensive backs their proper attacking courses with the defensive end's attacking route.

5. We want our defenders to come under control just prior to attacking the ball carrier so all of our defenders will have their proper balance.

Coaching Points:

Teaches the deep defenders their proper attacking courses and not to under or overrun the ball carrier.

Index